Workbook

Niall Boyle

Mentor Books Ltd
43 Furze Road
Sandyford Industrial Estate
Dublin 18
Republic of Ireland
Tel: +353 1 295 2112/3 Fax: +353 1 295 2114
e-mail: admin@mentorbooks.ie www.mentorbooks.ie

A catalogue record for this book is available from the British Library.

ISBN 978-1-909417-14-4

Editor: Deirdre O'Neill
Artwork: Brian Fitzgerald
Cover design and layout: Mary Byrne

Printed in Ireland by W&G Baird Ltd
1 3 5 7 9 10 8 6 4 2

Contents

Acknowledgements

The publishers would like to thank:

Alamy; Bridgeman Art; Getty Images; and Nelson Thornes.

The publishers have made every effort to trace and acknowledge the holders of copyright for material used in the book. In the event of a copyright holder having been overlooked, the publishers will come to a suitable arrangement at the first opportunity.

Where images from actual examination papers were difficult to source, the publishers have substituted alternatives.

ASSESSMENT

Introduction

In a school where **Religious Education** is offered as an examination subject, assessment has **two** elements:

- A written examination.
- A pre-submitted journal work booklet.

This applies to both **Higher Level** and **Ordinary Level**.

There are **500 marks** available in total at both Higher Level and Ordinary Level:

- **The examination paper** is worth 80 per cent of the total, i.e. **400 marks**.
- **The journal work booklet** is worth 20 per cent of the total, i.e. **100 marks**.

The Examination Paper

The examination paper can be taken at either **Higher Level** or **Ordinary Level**. In both cases:

- The examination is two hours long.
- A maximum of 400 marks may be awarded.

At Higher Level the examination paper has **five** sections. At Ordinary Level the examination paper has **four** sections.

Read the following charts. They will tell you:

- The marks given for each section of the examination paper.
- The time you should spend on each section.
- The different kinds of questions asked in each section.
- The number of questions you must answer in each section.

Higher Level Marking Scheme – Total Marks = 400

Section	Question type	Marks available	Time (minutes)	Number of questions	Number to answer
1	One-line/ tick box	50	15	20	Any 10
2	Image-based	30	15	4	Any 3
3	Comprehension	50	15	4	All
4	Detailed explanation	200	55	6	Any 4
5	Short essay	70	20	6	Any 1

Ordinary Level Marking Scheme – Total Marks = 400

Section	Question type	Marks available	Time (minutes)	Number of questions	Number to answer
1	One-line / tick box	80	20	20	Any 10
2	Image-based	60	20	4	Any 3
3	Comprehension	60	20	5	All
4	Detailed explanation	200	60	6	Any 5

The Journal Booklet

The journal work booklet is a document that is provided by the **State Examinations Commission (SEC)**. You must complete this document whether you are taking Higher Level or Ordinary Level. A maximum of 100 marks may be awarded.

You must choose one topic from a list of twelve titles. The titles are the same for both Higher Level and Ordinary Level.

You must do research on your chosen topic and write an essay on it. Then you must submit a report on your topic. This report is written into your journal booklet.

Cues/prompts are provided in the booklet to help you stay focused on the title of your chosen topic.

Your finished booklet is submitted for assessment along with your examination paper.

You have the option of doing this work either on your own or as a member of a class group. However, you must submit an individual journal booklet for assessment, outlining only your own contribution.

KNOW YOUR KEY IDEAS

Action of religious significance	Something you do to show that you have faith in God.
Afterlife	Belief in life after death.
Agnosticism	Belief that there is no way for us to know whether or not God exists.
Atheism	Belief that there is no God.
Atonement	Healing your relationship with God and with other people.
Authority	Either the power to make decisions on behalf of other people or a trusted source of guidance.
Belief	Something you accept as true.
Blasphemy	To show great disrespect for God by what you say or do.
Calendar	How we organise the year by dividing it up into days, weeks and months.
Code	Set of rules that tells you how you should behave towards others.
Commitment	Promise to give the time and energy needed to complete a task.
Common good	What is in the best interest of all members of a community.
Community	Where people choose to come together to do something they think is good or worthwhile, such as live, work or worship together.
Community of faith	A group of people who share a common set of beliefs about the meaning of life.
Conflict with authority	To openly challenge or disagree with the leaders of your community.
Conscience	Your capacity to apply your knowledge and values and decide what is the right thing to do.
Constitution	Document that sets out the ideas on which a state is based and the values that its people want to see reflected in its laws.
Cooperate	To work together.
Covenant	Sacred agreement between God and people.
Conversion	Completely changing how you think about and act towards God.
Creation	Action of God that brought the universe and all living things into existence.
Creed	Prayer that sets out the beliefs that are shared by all the members of a religion.
Death	Permanent ending of all the bodily functions that keep you alive.
Decision	A choice either to do or not to do something.
Denomination	Particular branch of a religious tradition.
Discern	To realise something or to figure something out.

Disciple	A follower or student of someone.
Document of faith	Source of information about a founder written by a member of that religion.
Document of history	Source of information about a founder written by someone who is not a member of that religion.
Dogma	Essential teaching that must be accepted by all members of a particular religion.
Ecumenism	Movement that encourages greater understanding and unity among the different Christian traditions.
Encounter with mystery	Being brought face to face with important questions about the meaning of life.
Enlightenment	Deep understanding of the meaning of life.
Environment	The world and everything in it: air, soil, water, plants, animals and humans.
Experience wonder	To encounter something so mysterious and unexpected that it demands your attention and respect.
Faith	Putting your trust in someone or something.
Festival	Religious celebration where people come together to praise and thank God.
Forgive	Letting go of the anger and hate you feel towards anyone who has harmed you or a loved one.
Founder	One who first set up a particular religion.
Golden rule	Always treat others as you would want them to treat you.
God	The Supreme Being, who created and sustains the universe.
Grace	The love and strength God gives to those who have faith in him.
Guidance	Advice about what is the best thing for you to do.
Guilt	Awareness that you have done something wrong and should be held accountable for it.
Honesty	Being fair and forthright in your dealings, keeping your word and telling the truth.
Human rights	Things we are entitled to because we are human beings. We need them to live free and full lives.
Hypocrite	Someone who pretends to be good but is not.
Idolatry	Worship of anyone or anything other than God.
Illegal	Something forbidden by the law.
Identity	What makes you different from everyone else.
Image of God	Picture of God you have in your mind.
Inspiring vision	Message of hope a founder preaches that leads others to follow him.
Integrity	Staying true to your beliefs, following your conscience and doing what you believe is right.

Inter-faith dialogue	Where members of the different religions meet to pray and talk with one another.
Judgement	When you are held accountable by God for how you have lived your life.
Justice	Getting what you are entitled to and giving others what they are entitled to.
Just war	One where there are good reasons to support taking military action.
Law	Rule set out by the state authorities that all its citizens are obliged to obey.
Leader	Someone who guides and motivates others towards achieving a particular goal.
Legal	Something permitted by the law.
Libertarianism	Belief that we should each be as free as possible to think, speak and act as we choose, so long as we do not interfere with the equal right of others to do the same.
Martyr	Someone who is prepared to die for what he/she believes is right.
Meditation	Way of finding the inner peace needed to let you focus your mind on finding answers to important questions in your life.
Memorial	Anything that recalls and shows respect for a person or event in the past.
Messiah	Someone sent by God to save you.
Metanoia	Complete change in your whole outlook on life.
Ministry	Serving others by playing a constructive role in your community.
Miracle	Wonderful and awe-inspiring event that has only one explanation: God did it.
Missionary	Someone who sets out to convert others to his/her religious faith.
Monotheism	Belief that there is only one God.
Moral evil	Harm caused when you freely and deliberately choose to do what you know is wrong.
Moral growth	Way in which you grow into someone who knows right from wrong.
Moral immaturity	Where you do not accept your responsibilities as a member of a community.
Moral maturity	Where you do accept your responsibilities as a member of a community.
Moral vision	Your own personal idea of what is right and wrong. It motivates you to think and act in certain ways.
Morality	Set of standards you use to judge whether an action is right or wrong.

Mystery	Something so vast and complex that it is beyond our capacity to ever completely figure out and solve.
Needs	Things we must have to live a fully human life.
Non-religious worldview	Belief that we can find happiness and fulfilment in our lives without belief in God or an afterlife.
Organised religion	One that has its own leaders, teachings and forms of worship.
Parable	Easily remembered story that uses examples drawn from every-day life to help us understand an important idea.
Participate in worship	To play an active role in worship.
Peace	Where people live together in a spirit of cooperation, fairness, honesty, justice and tolerance.
Periods of preparation	Times when the members of a religion fast and pray before a religious festival begins, e.g. Lent for Christians.
Personal prayer	When you pray alone.
Pilgrim	Someone who goes on a pilgrimage.
Pilgrimage	Spiritual journey made to a place of religious significance.
Place of religious significance	Somewhere important to the members of a particular religion, e.g. a site associated with some event in the life of that religion's founder.
Pluralism	Belief that all points of view, religious and non-religious, should be treated with equal respect. The laws of the state should reflect this belief by showing no favouritism towards any one community of faith.
Polytheism	Belief that there are many different gods.
Prayer	Way of focusing your attention on, and communicating with, God.
Preach	To teach or to explain.
Prejudice	Making up your mind about someone or something before finding out the facts or by ignoring the facts altogether.
Preside	To lead the community in worship.
Problem	Something we can figure out and solve.
Progress	Improvement in some area of life.
Prophet	Someone who receives messages from God and then passes them on to others.
Racism	Hostile attitude towards people of races other than your own.
Reflection	Stopping to think about the meaning of life and the direction your life is taking.
Reincarnation	Belief that when your current body dies, your soul will pass on into a new body and begin a new life here on earth.
Relationships	The different ways in which we are connected to or involved in each other's lives.
Religion	A way of life that is centred around belief in and worship of God.

Religious beliefs	Teachings about God and the meaning of life that the members of a religion accept as true.
Religious commitment	Making your best effort to live according to the teachings of your religion.
Religious faith	Putting your trust in God because you believe that God loves you and only wants what is best for you.
Religious festivals	Times that celebrate important events in the history of a religion, e.g. Passover for Jews.
Religious fundamentalism	Belief that a sacred text must be accepted as factually correct in every detail and understood literally.
Religious identity	Those beliefs, practices and symbols that clearly distinguish one religion from another.
Religious indifference	Complete lack of interest in anything to do with religious faith.
Religious practices	Different ways in which you express your religious beliefs through what you say and do.
Religious ritual	Where the members of a religion say and do the same things when they come together to worship as a community.
Repentance	To be truly sorry for the sins you have committed.
Respect	Showing that you care by the way you behave.
Responsible	Having to answer for how you have behaved.
Resurrection	When Jesus Christ rose from the dead to a new and glorious life that is eternal.
Revelation	When God reaches out to human beings and tells us important things that we could never know if left to our own efforts.
Role	Specific job that you do or the contribution you can make to your community.
Rule	Clear instruction as to how you should behave.
Sacrament	Religious ritual instituted by Jesus Christ in which God gives his love and strength to those who believe in him.
Sacred	Someone or something worthy of your total respect.
Sacred text	The holy book of a particular religion. It contains the most important stories and key teachings of that religion.
Sacrifice	Something given out of love to achieve something important.
Schism	A split within a religion.
Science	Knowledge of how the world works.
Sectarianism	Hostile attitude towards anyone who does not share your beliefs or way of life.
Sermon	Explanation of religious teachings.
Service	Action that helps us fulfil our human needs.
Sharing	Dividing things fairly so that we all have what we need.
Shrine	Monument that commemorates an important religious event.
Sign	Any image, word or gesture that communicates one and only one idea.

Sin	A freely chosen action where you deliberately do something you know is wrong or refuse to do something you know is right.
Socialisation	Way in which you learn what is meant by right and wrong, and develop the ability to tell one from the other.
Soul	The lifeforce that animates your body. The invisible source of your capacity to think, choose and love. It is created by God and survives the death of your body.
Sources of our values	Those people and things that influence our standards of right and wrong.
State	Community of people organised under a government.
Steward	Someone who cares for the earth.
Symbol	Any image, word or gesture that communicates more than one idea.
Table fellowship	Sharing a meal with others in a spirit of compassion, equality and friendship.
Technological worldview	Belief that we should always be looking for better and faster ways of making and doing things.
Theocracy	Where a state is governed by laws based solely on the religious and moral vision of the ruling group.
Times of religious significance	Religious festivals or periods of preparation for them.
Tolerance	Respect for the beliefs of others, even though you do not share them yourself.
Tradition	Distinctive way of thinking about and practising your religious faith. It is passed down over the centuries from one generation to the next.
Value	Anyone or anything that you think is good, desirable, important or worthwhile.
Vision	Outlook on life or set of beliefs that motivates you to think and act in certain ways.
Vocation	Belief that you are called by God to do something worthwhile with your life.
Witness	Showing your love for God and for other people by the way you live your life.
Worldview	Your general outlook on life.
Worship	Any action which shows: you have faith in God; recognise that there is no one greater than God; and want to give thanks and praise to God.

Section A
Communities of Faith

PART 1: COMMUNITY

EXPLAIN IT!

1. To cooperate means to ______________________________
2. A community is where ______________________________

   ____
3. Needs are ______________________________
4. Respect means ______________________________
5. A role is ______________________________
6. A rule is ______________________________

MATCH IT!

Match each explanation in column B with the correct need in column A.
Fill in your answers in the spaces provided.

A NEEDS	B EXPLANATIONS
5. Self-fulfilment needs →	You need to have a healthy respect for yourself. You need to know that you are respected by others too.
4. Esteem needs →	You need to develop your particular talents. You need to become the kind of person you are meant to be.
3. Social needs →	You need a stable, orderly and secure place in which to live, love, learn and work.
2. Safety needs →	You need clean water, nourishing food, clothing, sleep and shelter. These are necessary for good health. They are your most basic needs. They must be taken care of first.
1. Bodily needs →	You need to be loved and wanted, to have a sense of belonging. This gives you self-confidence, as you know who you are and where you fit in.

A NEEDS	B EXPLANATIONS
5. Self-fulfilment needs →	
4. Esteem needs →	
3. Social needs →	
2. Safety needs →	
1. Bodily needs →	

PART 2: COMMUNITIES IN ACTION

EXPLAIN IT!

1. A commitment is ______________________________

____

2. A service is ______________________________

____

3. A vision is ______________________________

____

4. A leader is ______________________________

____

MATCH IT!

Match the service offered in column B with the organisation in column A. Fill in your answers in the spaces provided.

A ORGANISATION	B SERVICE
Alcoholics Anonymous	1 Supporting people suffering from depression.
Aware	2 Supporting people who have lost a loved one through suicide.
Bóthar	3 Caring for terminally ill people.
Console	4 Emergency medical aid to victims of man-made and/ or natural disasters.
Focus Ireland	5 High-quality mobility training and aftercare services to blind and visually impaired people.
Irish Guide Dogs for the Blind	6 Supporting people with an addiction to alcohol.
The Hospice Movement	7 Helping families in the developing world overcome hunger and poverty and restore the environment in a sustainable way.
The Red Cross	8 Working to combat and prevent homelessness.

A ORGANISATION	B SERVICE
Alcoholics Anonymous	
Aware	
Bóthar	
Console	
Focus Ireland	
Irish Guide Dogs for the Blind	
The Hospice Movement	
The Red Cross	

LOOK AND ANSWER!

(*From J/C, OL 2007*)

This is a photograph of a religious sister serving the needs of others.

A. Choose one thing from this photograph which shows that she is serving the needs of others.

____

B. Name one example of a community.

____

C. Give two reasons why we all need to live in a community.

(i) ______________________________

____

(ii) ______________________________

____

PART 3: COMMUNITIES OF FAITH

EXPLAIN IT!

1. A community of faith is ______________________________

____

2. Faith means______________________________

____

3. A religion is ______________________________

____

4. Monotheism is ______________________________

____

5. Polytheism is ______________________________

____

6. A religious identity is ______________________________

____

7. A religious symbol is ______________________________

____

8. A sacred text is ______________________________

____

9. Revelation is ______________________________

____

10. A founder is ______________________________

____

11. An inspiring vision is ______________________________

____

12. A creed is ______________________________

____

13. A schism is ______________________________

14. A religious commitment means ______________________________

____

15. A vocation is ______________________________

____

FILL IN THE SPACES!

Name	Founding date	Place founded	Followers called
Hinduism			
Judaism			
Buddhism			
Christianity			
Islam			

MATCH IT!

1. Read the list of sacred texts and the list of world religions given below. One sacred text has been matched to the world religion with which it is most associated as an example for you. Match the other ones.

A SACRED TEXT	B RELIGIONS
The Gospels	Buddhism
The Qur'an	Christianity
The Tenakh	Hinduism
The Tripitaka	Judaism
The Vedas	Islam

A SACRED TEXT	B RELIGIONS
The Gospels	Christianity
The Qur'an	
The Tenakh	
The Tripitaka	
The Vedas	

2. Read the lists of leaders and world religions given below. One leader has been matched to the religion with which he is most associated as an example for you. Match the other ones.

A LEADERS	B RELIGIONS
Brahmins/Rishis	Buddhism
Jesus	Islam
Moses	Hinduism
Muhammad	Christianity
Siddhartha Gautama	Judaism

A LEADERS	B RELIGIONS
Brahmins/Rishis	Hinduism
Jesus	
Moses	
Muhammad	
Siddhartha Gautama	

3. Match each denomination in column B with the correct tradition in column A. Fill in your answers in the spaces provided.

A TRADITION	B DENOMINATION
Catholic	Presbyterian
Orthodox	Church of Ireland
Anglican	Russian
Protestant	Roman rite

A TRADITION	B DENOMINATION
Catholic	Roman rite
Orthodox	
Anglican	
Protestant	

LOOK AND ANSWER!

This is a photograph of a person reading a sacred text.

A. Choose one thing from this photograph which suggests that this person is reading a sacred text.

____

____

B. Name one sacred text associated with a world religion you have studied.

____

____

C. State two teachings from the sacred text you have named.

____

____

THINK ABOUT IT!

(*From J/C 2009 HL*)

A. Give two reasons why belonging to a community of faith could be important for people.

(i) ______

(ii) ______

Communication ❑ Cooperation ❑

B. Choose one of the above and say why it is important for a community of faith.

______

PART 4: RELATIONSHIPS BETWEEN COMMUNITIES OF FAITH

EXPLAIN IT!

1. Sectarianism is ______

2. Pluralism says that ______

3. Inter-faith dialogue is ______

4. Tolerance means ______

5. Ecumenism is ______

LOOK AND ANSWER!

(*From J/C 2011*)

This is a photograph of people gathering for inter-faith dialogue.

A. Choose one thing from this photograph which suggests that it is an example of an inter-faith gathering.

____

____

B. Give another example of inter-faith dialogue.

____

____

C. Give two reasons why the members of a community of faith should take part in inter-faith dialogue.

(i) ______________________________

____

____

____

(ii) ______________________________

____

____

____

HL

PART 5: ORGANISATIONS AND LEADERSHIP IN COMMUNITIES OF FAITH

[Higher Level Only]

EXPLAIN IT!

1. Racism is ______________________________

____

2. Authority is ______________________________

____

3. Reincarnation is ______________________________

____

4. The pope is the leader of ______________________________

5. The Dalai Lama is the leader of ______________________________

LOOK AND ANSWER!

(*From J/C HL 2009*)

This is a photograph of members of a community of faith showing respect at the tomb of Pope John Paul II.

A. Choose one thing from this photograph which suggests that the members of this community of faith are showing respect at this tomb.

____

____

B. Give one other example of a way in which members of a community of faith can show respect.

____

____

C. State two reasons why showing respect is important for members of a community of faith.

(i) ______________________________

____

(ii) ______________________________

____

THINK ABOUT IT!

(*From J/C 2010*)

A. Name **one** religious leader associated with a community of faith in Ireland. (Suggestion: the Anglican Archbishop of Armagh)

____

B. Describe the work done by this religious leader in that community of faith.

____

____

____

____

WORDSEARCH

Find the following key ideas:

COMMITMENT
COMMUNICATION
COMMUNITY
DIALOGUE
FAITH
FOUNDER
IDENTITY
LEADER
MINISTRY
MONOTHEISM
NEEDS
RELIGION
RESPECT
REVELATION
ROLE
TOLERANCE

C	Y	L	F	X	K	C	M	N	F	T	O	V	K	S
M	O	T	H	N	L	F	E	J	J	C	R	S	C	E
R	I	M	I	V	K	A	I	N	M	E	G	D	M	I
F	E	N	M	N	T	A	C	S	L	P	M	N	Z	D
T	A	D	I	U	U	U	D	I	B	S	S	I	U	E
F	R	I	N	S	N	M	G	Y	U	E	I	L	I	N
I	Y	K	T	U	T	I	M	E	W	R	E	G	O	T
R	O	L	E	H	O	R	C	O	N	K	H	I	N	I
F	P	L	K	N	Q	F	Y	A	C	X	T	K	E	T
C	O	M	M	I	T	M	E	N	T	A	O	L	E	Y
D	I	A	L	O	G	U	E	D	L	I	N	G	D	T
R	E	D	A	E	L	R	L	E	T	F	O	R	S	R
S	S	L	Y	M	E	A	V	V	T	F	M	N	U	L
V	E	C	N	A	R	E	L	O	T	Z	Z	Y	J	J
A	Y	H	S	H	R	Z	B	D	Z	J	E	R	E	Z

SOLVE IT!

Clues

Across

3. Someone who guides and motivates you to achieve a goal.
6. Outlook on life that motivates you to act in certain ways.
10. Someone who sets up a religion.
13. Respect for the beliefs of others, even though you do not share them.
14. Means a split.
17. Believes there is only one God.
20. Christianity's sacred text.
21. Unpaid work serving the needs of others.

Down

1. A middle way between the Catholic and the Protestant traditions.
2. We must have them to live a fully human life.
4. Way of life centred on believe in and worship of God.
5. Means putting your trust in someone or something.
7. Encourages greater unity among the different Christian traditions.
8. God appeared to him in the form of a bush that was on fire but did not burn.
9. Leader of the Catholic Church.
11. Being called by God to do something worthwhile.
12. To show you care in what you say and do.
15. Where people choose to come together to do something they think is good or worthwhile.
16. Organisation founded by Anton Wallich-Clifford.
18. Prayer that sets out the beliefs shared by all members of a religion.
19. A clear instruction as to how you should behave.

Section B

Foundations of Religion - Christianity

PART 1: THE CONTEXT

EXPLAIN IT!

1. The Fertile Crescent was ______________________________

____

2. The Sanhedrin was ______________________________

____

3. Messiah means ______________________________

____

TICK THE BOX!

1. The Holy Land has the Mediterranean Sea on one side and the desert of Arabia on the other.

True ☐ False ☐

2. The Roman governor in Palestine at the time of Jesus was called:

Peter ☐ Philip ☐ Pilate ☐

3. Galilee was a province in Palestine at the time of Jesus.

True ☐ False ☐

4. Most Jews lived in large cities dotted across Palestine.

True ☐ False ☐

5. There was no fireplace in a typical Jewish home.

True ☐ False ☐

6. When a Jewish boy reached the age of thirteen he was publicly examined on his knowledge of the Tenakh.

True ☐ False ☐

7. The second Temple in Jerusalem was rebuilt and enlarged by Julius Caesar.

True ☐ False ☐

8. The only part of the Temple that is still standing is the Eastern Wall.

True ☐ False ☐

9. Tax collectors were treated as social outcasts by their fellow Jews.
True ☐ False ☐

10. The Sanhedrin was divided into two rival groups: the Sadducees and the Essenes.
True ☐ False ☐

11. The Sadducees expected a messiah to free them from Roman rule.
True ☐ False ☐

12. The Pharisees encouraged their fellow Jews to mix with non-Jews.
True ☐ False ☐

13. The Essenes set up monastic communities in remote parts of Palestine.
True ☐ False ☐

14. The Zealots believed that the messiah would be a mighty warrior who would free them from Roman rule.
True ☐ False ☐

MAP WORK!

1. Identify each of the following features of Palestine in the time of Jesus.

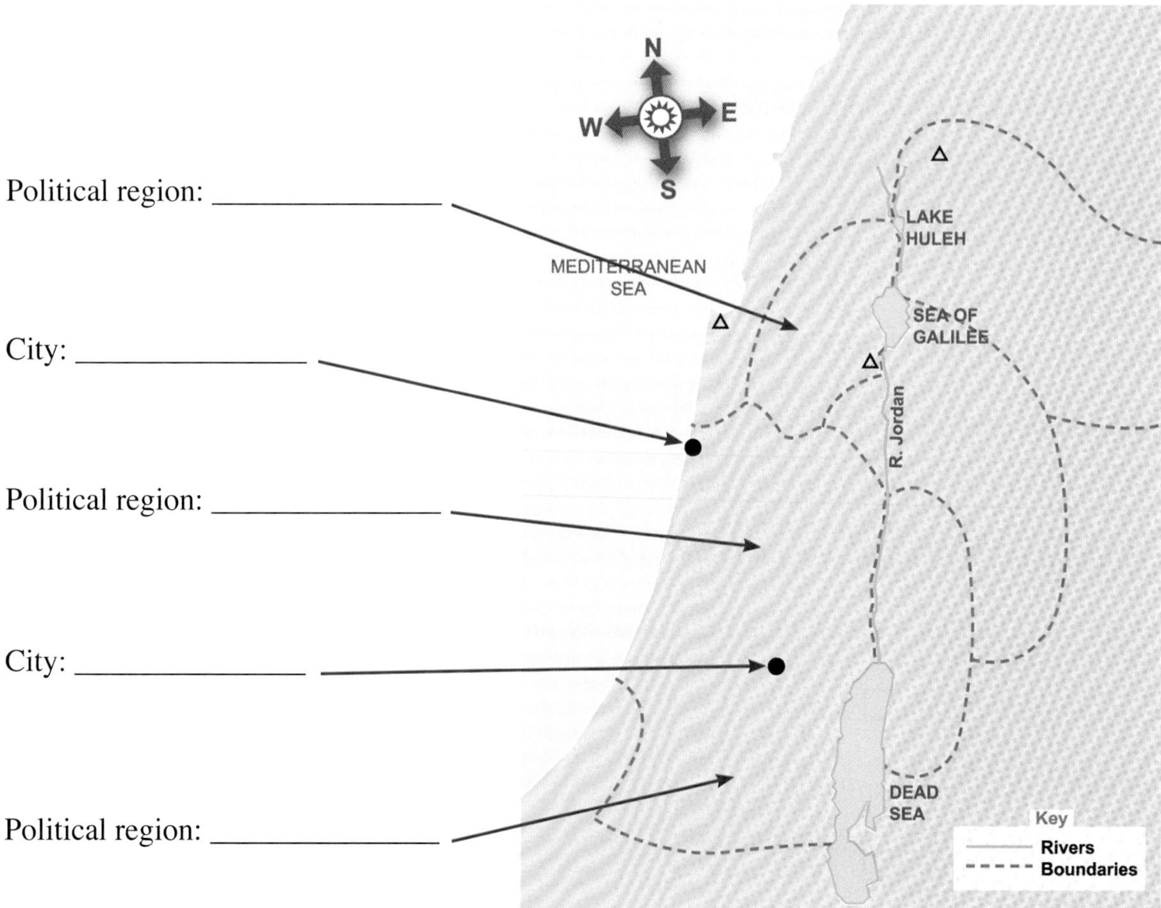

IDENTIFY THE KEY FEATURES!

1. Identify each of these features of the Temple in the time of Jesus.

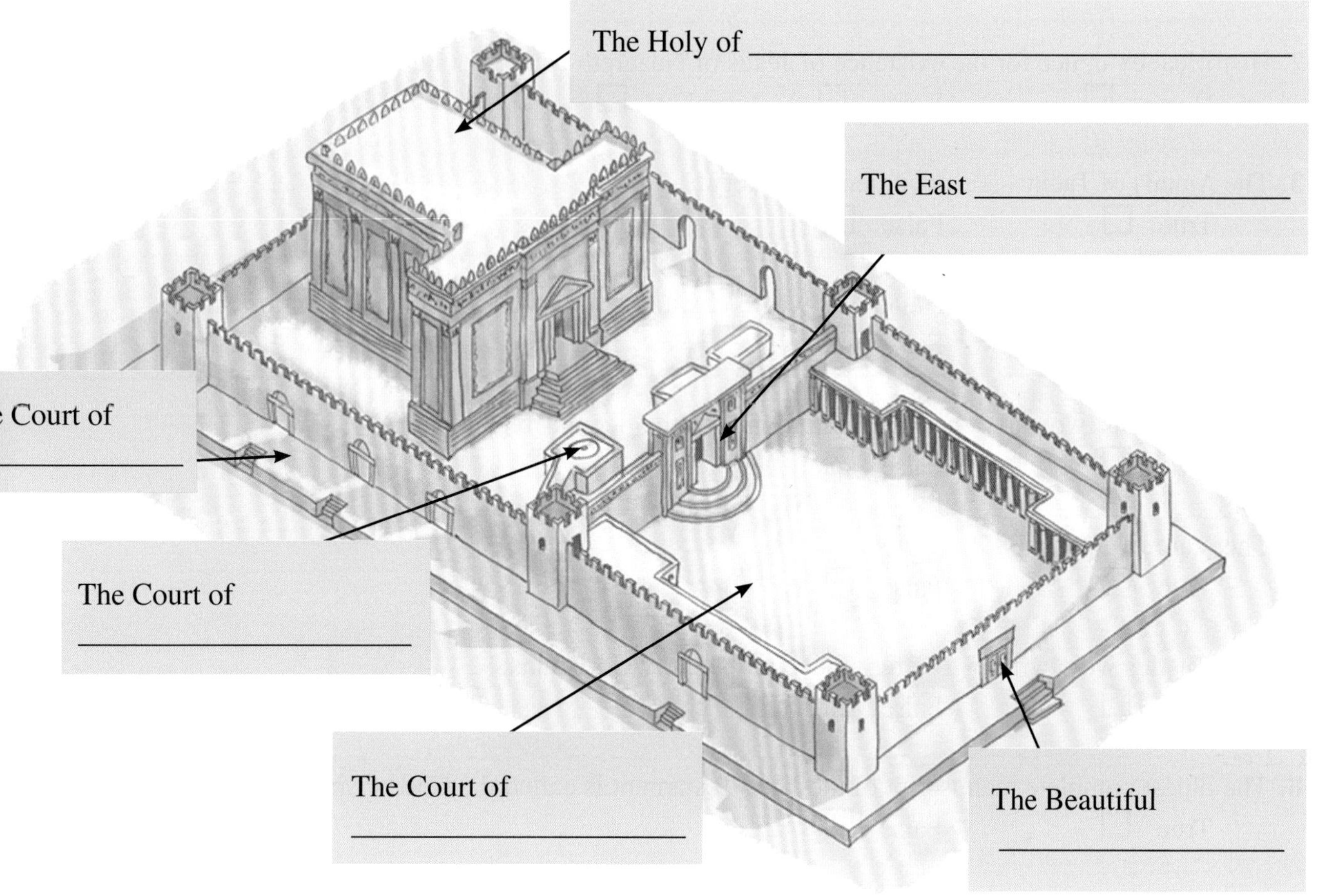

PART 2: EVIDENCE ABOUT JESUS

EXPLAIN IT!

1. A document of history is ________________________________
____

2. A document of faith is ________________________________
____

3. Gospel means ____

4. An evangelist is ______________________________________

TICK THE BOX!

1. Evidence is any kind of information that allows you to find out what happened in the past.
True ☐ False ☐

2. Historical evidence for the existence of Jesus of Nazareth can be found in the writings of:
Hosea ☐ Isaiah ☐ Josephus ☐

3. The Annals of Tacitus is a document of history.
True ☐ False ☐

4. The Letter to the Emperor Trajan was written by a Roman procurator named Pontius Pilate.
True ☐ False ☐

5. The Bible has two parts: the First Testament and the Second Testament.
True ☐ False ☐

6. There are five gospels.
True ☐ False ☐

7. The epistles were written to offer advice to the early Christians.
True ☐ False ☐

8. The oldest complete manuscript of the New Testament is called the Codex Sinaiticus.
True ☐ False ☐

9. The gospels are documents of faith.
True ☐ False ☐

10. The Gospel of Mark is a Synoptic Gospel.
True ☐ False ☐

11. The Gospel of John is a Synoptic Gospel.
True ☐ False ☐

12. Matthew was the last of the evangelists to write a gospel.
True ☐ False ☐

13. Jesus was born in the town of:
Nazareth ☐ Damascus ☐ Bethlehem ☐

14. Jesus was most likely born some time between 4 CE and 6 CE.
True ☐ False ☐

PART 3: THE PERSON AND PREACHING OF JESUS

EXPLAIN IT!

1. The public ministry of Jesus was ______________________________
____

2. Repentance means ____
____

3. A disciple is ____
____

4. A parable is ____
____

5. A miracle is ____
____

6. Blasphemy means ____
____

7. Table-fellowship means ____________________________________
____

TICK THE BOX!

1. Jesus grew up in the town of:
   Jericho ☐ Jerusalem ☐ Nazareth ☐

2. Jesus was baptised in the river:
   Ganges ☐ Jordan ☐ Nile ☐ Tiber ☐

3. Most Jews in the time of Jesus hoped that the messiah would set up an independent Jewish kingdom.
   True ☐ False ☐

4. The title 'rabbi' is most associated with a leader in which of the following world religions:
   Buddhism ☐ Hinduism ☐ Judaism ☐

5. Matthew was a tax collector before he became an apostle.
   True ☐ False ☐

6. A parable is a story with a deeper meaning contained within it.
   True ☐ False ☐

7. The first-century Jewish historian Josephus described Jesus as a miracle-worker.
True ☐ False ☐

8. The raising of Jairus's daughter is one example of a nature miracle.
True ☐ False ☐

9. The cure of the man born blind is one example of a healing miracle.
True ☐ False ☐

10. Jesus healed the paralysed man to show the Pharisees that he had the power to forgive sins.
True ☐ False ☐

11. A patriarchal society is one where women and men are treated as equals.
True ☐ False ☐

12. The Pharisees agreed with Jesus about sharing meals with the poor, outcasts and gentiles.
True ☐ False ☐

13. Jesus sharing a meal with Zacchaeus the tax collector is an example of table-fellowship.
True ☐ False ☐

MATCH IT!

Match the correct example in column B with the type of miracle listed in column A.

A TYPE OF MIRACLE	B EXAMPLE
Healing miracle	The raising of Lazarus (John 11:38–44)
Exorcism (i.e. casting out demons)	The man born blind (John 9:1–41)
Nature miracle	The demon-possessed man (Mark 5:1–20)
Restoration to life	The calming of the storm (Matthew 8:23–27)

Fill in your answers in the spaces provided below.

A TYPE OF MIRACLE	B EXAMPLE
Healing miracle	
Exorcism (i.e. casting out demons)	
Nature miracle	
Restoration to life	

LOOK AND ANSWER!

(J/C 2010)

This drawing is based on Jesus calling his disciples.

A. Pick one thing from the drawing which suggests that it is based on Jesus calling his disciples.

____

____

____

____

B. Name **one** person Jesus called to be his disciple.

____

State **two** things that Jesus asked his disciples to do.

(i) ______________________________

____

(ii) ______________________________

____

PART 4: THE DEATH AND RESURRECTION OF JESUS

EXPLAIN IT!

1. Holy Week was ____

____

2. A conflict with authority is ___________________________________

____

3. A memorial is ____

____

4. The passion of Jesus was ____________________________________

____

5. A martyr is ____

____

6. Crucifixion was ____

____

7. A sacrifice is ____

____

8. The resurrection was ____

____

TICK THE BOX!

1. Jesus arrived in Jerusalem on the Sunday of Holy Week and was greeted by crowds waving palm branches.

True ☐ False ☐

2. On the Monday of Holy Week Jesus drove the money-changers out of the Antonia Fortress.

True ☐ False ☐

3. Simon Peter betrayed Jesus to his enemies in the Sanhedrin.

True ☐ False ☐

4. After the Last Supper, Jesus went to pray in the Garden of Gethsemane.

True ☐ False ☐

5. The high priest who interrogated Jesus was named Caiaphas.
True ☐ False ☐

6. Judas denied ever knowing Jesus three times.
True ☐ False ☐

7. Jesus was sentenced to death by Pontius Pilate.
True ☐ False ☐

8. The crucifixion of Jesus is most associated with the following place:
Gaza ☐ Gilgal ☐ Golgotha ☐

9. The day of the week on which Jesus died was:
Easter Sunday ☐ Good Friday ☐ Holy Thursday ☐

10. The first person the risen Jesus appeared to was Mary Magdalene.
True ☐ False ☐

11. The apostles immediately accepted the news that Jesus had risen from the dead.
True ☐ False ☐

12. Ascension is a Christian religious festival that celebrates:
Jesus returning to his Father in heaven ☐ Jesus rising from the dead ☐ The Apostles receiving the Holy Spirit ☐

LOOK AND ANSWER!

(J/C 2012)

This picture is based on a Gospel account of the resurrection of Jesus.

1. Pick **one** thing from this picture which suggests that it is based on the resurrection of Jesus.

____

____

2. On which of the following days of the week did the disciples of Jesus first discover his resurrection?

Friday ☐ Saturday ☐ Sunday ☐

3. State **two** ways in which the first Christians were affected by the resurrection of Jesus.

(i) ____

____

(ii) ____

____

READ AND ANSWER!

Read the following article and answer all the questions that follow.

Oscar Romero – Christian Martyr

Oscar Romero was appointed head of the Catholic Church in El Salvador at a time when it was a place of great poverty and suffering for many people. The wealth of the country was controlled by a small number of people who were supported by the army. Many attempts to improve the conditions of the poor were put down by violence. Romero felt called to follow the example of Jesus Christ and speak out on behalf of the poor. Whenever he saw that the human rights of people were not being respected, he spoke out and demanded explanations from the government. He encouraged public protests against injustice and urged people to protest peacefully, saying, 'Only evil profits by murder.'

Oscar Romero used his position as a church leader to tell the world about what was happening in El Salvador. He opened his home to people who were trying to get away from the violence and allowed a radio station to be set up in the office of the cathedral. The radio station made it possible for people all over the country to listen each week to the sermons Romero preached about the rights of the poor. His sermons were often critical of the government and gave comfort to the people who were suffering because of the injustice and violence in the country.

Oscar Romero knew that his life was being put at risk by speaking out against injustice. He said, 'My life has been threatened many times…I am obliged to give my life for those I love…for the people of El Salvador.'

On 23 March 1980 Oscar Romero used the radio broadcast of his sermon to appeal for all those involved in violence to stop the killing in El Salvador.

The day after he made this appeal, Romero was shot dead by a gunman while celebrating the Eucharist.

Adapted from www.cafod.org.uk and Veritas Publications

1. Outline how this article shows what is meant by each of the following terms:

(**a**) Martyrdom

____

____

(**b**) Mission

____

____

2. Describe another example of how **either** martyrdom **or** mission can be seen in a community of faith you have studied.

____

____

____

____

3. (**a**) **Buddhism** ☐ **Christianity** ☐ **Hinduism** ☐ **Islam** ☐ **Judaism** ☐

Oscar Romero is one example of a person of faith who has inspired others. Name **another** person, associated with one of the world religions listed above, whose faith has inspired others.

____

(**b**) Outline how the religious faith of the person you have named above can be seen in an event from his/her life.

____

____

____

____

THINK ABOUT IT!

(J/C 2008)

A. (**i**) Below you will find a list of some of the events leading up to the death of Jesus. Number these events in the order in which they occurred. **Number 1** should be the first event and **Number 5** should be the last event.

Number	Event
	The Crucifixion
	Jesus is brought before Pontius Pilate
	Jesus is brought before the Sanhedrin
	The Last Supper
	Temple guards arrest Jesus

(ii) Describe the role of the Roman procurator in Palestine at the time of Jesus.

(iii) Who held the position of procurator during the public ministry of Jesus?

B. Imagine you were one of the disciples. You witnessed Jesus's death and were present when Jesus appeared after his resurrection.

(i) Describe the impact that the death of Jesus had on your life.

(ii) Describe one of the appearances of the risen Jesus you witnessed and the effect it had on you.

PART 5: FAITH IN CHRIST

EXPLAIN IT!

1. Pentecost was

2. The name Jesus Christ means

3. The name Christian means

4. A Christian missionary is

5. Conversion means

6. Heresy means

7. A convert is

8. The people of God means

9. An organised religion is ____

____

10. The Trinity is ____

____

TICK THE BOX!

1. The symbols of wind and fire were used by the evangelist Luke to convey the idea of the Holy Spirit descending on the disciples at Pentecost.
True ☐ False ☐

2. Stephen was the last Christian martyr in Jerusalem.
True ☐ False ☐

3. The apostle Peter was put to death in India.
True ☐ False ☐

4. Thomas is said to have been the only apostle who lived to old age and died of natural causes.
True ☐ False ☐

5. The Jews living outside Palestine were known as the diaspora.
True ☐ False ☐

6. A mission is a particular job that you have agreed to do.
True ☐ False ☐

7. In 35 CE Paul underwent a dramatic conversion to Judaism while travelling on the road to Damascus.
True ☐ False ☐

8. Paul's epistles were letters offering advice to the new Christian communities that were being set up around the Roman Empire.
True ☐ False ☐

9. Paul was martyred in Jerusalem on the orders of the Emperor Tiberius.
True ☐ False ☐

10. The Council of Jerusalem decided that all you needed to become a Christian was repentance of your sins and baptism.
True ☐ False ☐

11. The early Christians agreed to worship the Roman emperor.
True ☐ False ☐

12. In 313 CE the Emperor Constantine granted Christians freedom of worship.
True ☐ False ☐

13. The Son of God was the only specific title that Jesus is recorded as having directly applied to himself.
True ☐ False ☐

14. The Jews believed that God's name was so holy that it should never be spoken aloud.
True ☐ False ☐

15. The Incarnation means God made human.
True ☐ False ☐

LOOK AND ANSWER!

(J/C 2009)

This picture is based on the first Christians' experience of Pentecost.

1. Pick one thing from this picture which shows that it is based on the first Christians' experience of Pentecost.

____

____

2. The first Christians experienced Pentecost after the death of Jesus.
True ☐ False ☐

3. State **two** effects the experience of Pentecost had on the first Christians.

(i) ______________________________

____

(ii) ______________________________

____

WORDSEARCH

Find the following key ideas:

PALESTINE
PROCURATOR
SANHEDRIN
MESSIAH
SADDUCEE
PHARISEE
ESSENE
ZEALOT
BIBLE
GOSPEL
DISCIPLE
MIRACLE
FELLOWSHIP
MARTYR
CRUCIFIXION
RESURRECTION
ASCENSION

A	M	X	Y	H	A	I	S	S	E	M	M	F	Q	W
T	U	V	O	S	N	P	Y	N	T	E	A	R	Y	D
W	L	F	K	H	V	H	T	I	W	E	R	M	B	C
T	B	E	L	B	I	B	O	R	J	C	E	N	S	R
P	W	L	E	K	S	T	L	D	R	U	S	O	P	U
A	G	L	G	L	O	F	A	E	C	D	U	I	X	C
L	U	O	E	W	P	W	E	H	U	D	R	S	O	I
E	P	W	S	W	I	I	Z	N	I	A	R	N	T	F
S	H	S	S	P	L	J	C	A	G	S	E	E	S	I
T	A	H	E	G	E	G	T	S	N	H	C	C	U	X
I	R	I	N	I	Y	L	U	K	I	W	T	S	S	I
N	I	P	E	H	C	E	Z	Q	H	D	I	A	L	O
E	S	E	P	R	O	C	U	R	A	T	O	R	U	N
J	E	R	M	A	R	T	Y	R	I	N	N	G	Z	A
W	E	Y	W	V	W	M	I	R	A	C	L	E	C	S

SOLVE IT!

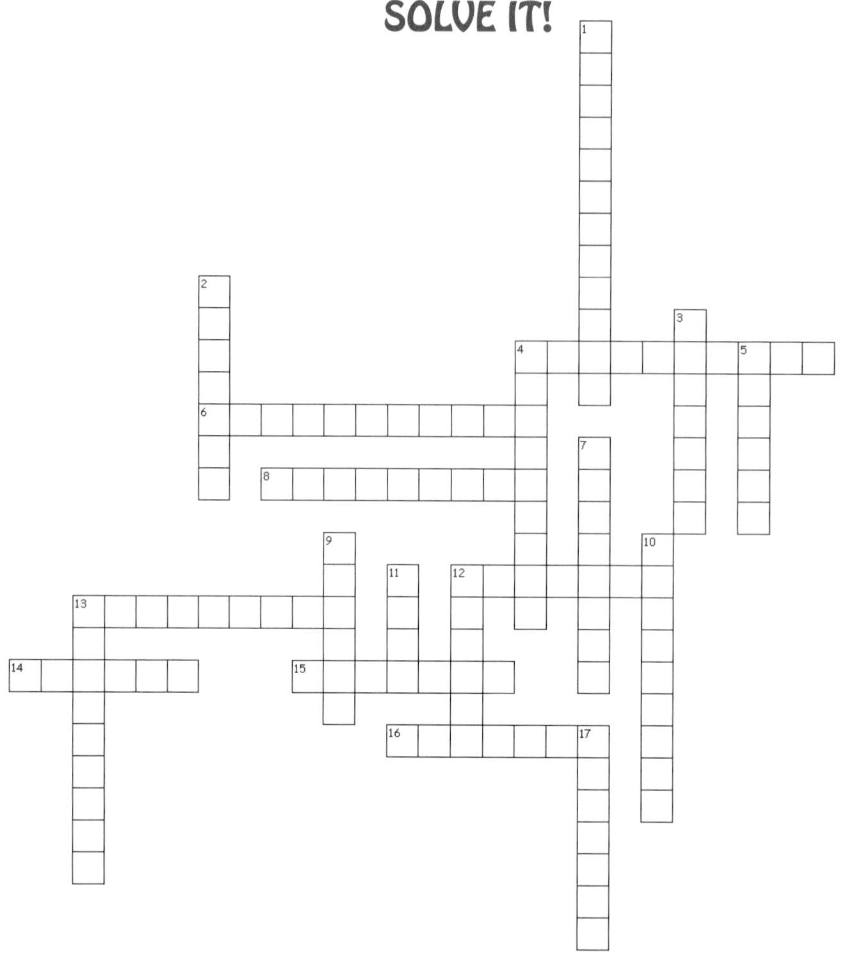

Clues

Across

4. Means a Roman governor.

6. Method of execution used on non-Romans.

8. Name of a province of the Roman Empire in the time of Jesus.

12. Title of saviour sent by God to free the Jews.

13. Wealthy landowners and priests who cooperated with the Romans.

14. Name of Judaism's sacred text.

15. Group violently opposed to Roman rule.

16. An easily remembered story drawn from everyday life containing an important message.

Down

1. When Jesus rose from the dead to a new and glorious life.

2. Event that can only be explained by saying God did it.

3. Christian belief that there are three divine persons in the one God.

4. When the disciples received the gifts of the Holy Spirit.

5. Holy land's most sacred building in the time of Jesus.

7. Means 'follower of Jesus'.

9. Means 'good news'.

10. Laymen who controlled the synagogues.

11. Most outstanding Christian missionary of the first century.

12. Someone ready to die for what he or she believes is right.

13. Ruling council of the Jewish religion.

17. Called themselves 'the Sons of Light'.

Section C
Foundations of Religion - Islam

EXPLAIN IT!

1. Islam means ______________________________

____

2. Muslim means ______________________________

____

3. The Ka'bah is ______________________________

4. The Qur'an is ______________________________

____

5. The Hadith is ______________________________

6. The Sunnah is ______________________________

____

7. A prophet is ______________________________

____

8. Salat is ______________________________

____

9. Zakat is ______________________________

____

10. Saum is ______________________________

____

11. The Hajj is ______________________________

____

12. A mosque is ______________________________

____

13. Shirk means ______________________________

____

14. Aqiqa is ______________________________

15. Caliph means ______________________________

16. The Umma is ______________________________

TICK THE BOX!

1. Muslims believe in one God, whom they call:
Allah ☐ Buddha ☐ Yahweh ☐

2. Muslims say that the Ka'bah was the first house on earth.
True ☐ False ☐

3. The name Muhammad means 'highly praised'.
True ☐ False ☐

4. The angel Jibril appeared to Muhammad in a cave on Mount Sinai.
True ☐ False ☐

5. A prophet is someone who receives messages from God which he passes on to others.
True ☐ False ☐

6. Muhammad demanded that all idols be removed from the Ka'bah.
True ☐ False ☐

7. The Ka'bah sits at the centre of the al-Masjid al-Haram mosque in Makkah.
True ☐ False ☐

8. The Qur'an is written in Arabic.
True ☐ False ☐

9. All Muslims must accept the Six Articles of Faith.
True ☐ False ☐

10. A Muslim must go on pilgrimage to Makkah at least twice in a lifetime.
True ☐ False ☐

11. Muslims worship only God. They do not worship Muhammad.
True ☐ False ☐

12. A madrasah is an Islamic school.
True ☐ False ☐

13. The imam calls Muslims to prayer from a minaret.
True ☐ False ☐

14. The khatib preaches the sermon in the mosque on Friday.
True ☐ False ☐

15. According to the Hadith, Muslims must pray seven times each day.
True ☐ False ☐

16. Attendance at Saturday prayers in the mosque is compulsory for Muslims.
True ☐ False ☐

17. The Qur'an forbids Muslims from drawing an image of Allah.
True ☐ False ☐

18. All pilgrims to Makkah must wear the ihram.
True ☐ False ☐

19. Ramadan is the twelfth month of the Muslim calendar.
True ☐ False ☐

20. Eid-ul-Fitr marks the end of the Hajj.
True ☐ False ☐

21. The Shia make up about 90 per cent of the worldwide Islamic community.
True ☐ False ☐

MATCH IT!

Match each name in column **B** with the correct **Pillar of Faith** listed in column **A**. Fill in your answers in the spaces provided.

A PILLAR OF FAITH	B NAME OF PILLAR
First Pillar	Saum
Second Pillar	Hajj
Third Pillar	Shahadah
Fourth Pillar	Salat
Fifth Pillar	Zakat

A PILLAR OF FAITH	B NAME OF PILLAR
First Pillar	
Second Pillar	
Third Pillar	
Fourth Pillar	
Fifth Pillar	

READ AND ANSWER!

Read the following article and answer all the questions that follow.

A Young Muslim's Experience of the Hajj

I was fifteen years old when I went on the Hajj. Nothing could have prepared me for the sight that met me when I first arrived at the holy city of Makkah. I could not believe how many Muslim brothers and sisters there were. Everywhere you looked, there were thousands upon thousands of men and women, of all races and all speaking different languages. My father told me that in total there were probably about two million pilgrims from all around the world here for the Hajj.

Then we began the rituals and journey of the Hajj. Everyone was dressed in the pilgrims' clothes of ihram, which is a white garment. You spend all of Hajj in ihram, which means that you are cleansing your soul of sin. The sight of two million Muslims all dressed in ihram was really special. When it came to prayer, the noise of all of us praising Allah in Arabic was something I will always hear and remember. When I was standing, shoulder to shoulder with my eyes shut in prayer with African, American and other Muslims, all I could hear was one voice together – no accents or different languages.

For the rest of the eleven days on pilgrimage, we all moved together, slept in the same tents and shared the same food. It was easy to forget where I was from, and being British was unimportant during the Hajj, because I was a Muslim there, the same as everyone else. It was the most fantastic experience of my life. It taught me a lot about looking beyond people's appearances and differences, which I often see people fail to do at home and at school. The Prophet Muhammad (peace be upon him) once said, 'All of you descend from Adam', and on the Hajj it really felt like we were all one because we shared the same beliefs and values. Nobody is more important than anyone else.

Adapted from Exploring Questions in Religious Education 2, G.Davies and M. Davies (Nelson Thornes, 2005)

1. What is the Hajj? ______________________________

____

2. State **two** reasons why Muslims go on pilgrimage.

(i) ______________________________

____

(ii) ______________________________

____

3. Identify two things that show that everyone is equal while taking part in the Hajj.

(i) ______________________________

____

(ii) ______________________________

____

4. Identify one important lesson that this young Muslim pilgrim learned from going on the Hajj.

____

____

THINK ABOUT IT!

(J/C 2008)

A. (i) People of faith gather to mark key moments in life such as birth, death and so on. Name **one** religious ceremony that marks an important moment in the life of a Muslim.

____

(ii) Outline what happens during the religious ceremony you have named above.

____

____

____

____

B. (i) What is the name given to the building where Muslims regularly gather for prayer?

____

(ii) Describe **two** ways in which the place you have named helps believers to pray.

1. ____

____

2. ____

____

WORDSEARCH

Find the following key ideas:

ALLAH
AQIQA
CALIPH
EID
HADITH
HAJJ
HIJRAH
HIRA
IMAM
KABAH
MADINAH
MAKKAII
MINARET
MOSQUE
MOUNT
MUHAMMAD
PROPHET
QURAN
RAMADAN
RASUL
SHIA
SUNNI
WUDU

A	C	L	R	U	J	I	M	A	M	N	J	X	T	M
D	L	O	U	M	H	E	M	F	A	J	C	N	U	I
Q	I	L	L	I	A	Y	B	D	A	P	U	H	D	S
N	C	E	A	H	K	D	A	H	S	O	A	B	V	C
W	A	V	U	H	K	M	I	U	M	M	L	C	I	A
D	B	R	D	I	A	T	N	N	M	B	U	R	C	L
H	E	V	U	R	M	N	O	A	A	F	S	F	F	I
P	A	L	J	Q	I	S	D	C	V	H	A	M	V	P
R	I	R	V	M	E	W	M	I	N	A	R	E	T	H
O	H	X	J	M	Y	J	H	N	N	J	L	M	T	W
P	S	Z	H	I	O	G	I	W	E	Q	O	A	V	N
H	T	I	D	A	H	B	R	P	U	S	A	S	G	P
E	Z	X	Z	K	A	B	A	H	Q	D	I	I	I	N
T	H	V	A	Q	I	Q	A	U	C	I	U	Y	T	A
I	S	B	O	K	T	E	E	B	V	N	J	M	I	S

SOLVE IT!

Clues

Across

2. Title of Islam's sacred text.
7. The name of the second pillar.
8. Muslim naming ritual.
9. Name of God according to Islam.
10. Plain white garment worn by Muslim pilgrims.
12. He calls Muslims to prayer.
14. Islam's holiest shrine. Name means 'the house of God'.
15. Someone who receives messages from God and passes them on to people.
16. The name of the first pillar.
18. Name given to the worldwide Islamic community.
19. Name of the holy well in Makkah.

Down

1. Collection of stories about Muhammad.
3. Means 'successor'.
4. Every surah begins with it.
5. Collection of Muhammad's sayings.
6. Pilgrimage all Muslims must make once in a lifetime.
11. Means 'a place of prostration'.
13. Arabic word for festival.
14. He preaches the sermon at prayers on Friday.
17. The departure of the Muslim community from Makkah to Madinah.
20. His name means 'highly praised'.

Section D

The Question of Faith

PART 1: THE SITUATION OF FAITH TODAY

EXPLAIN IT!

1. Religious beliefs are ____

____

2. Religious practices are ____

____

TICK THE BOX!

1. Nine out of ten countries in the world that have the lowest levels of belief in God are in Asia.
True ☐ False ☐

2. Around 13 per cent of Europeans call themselves atheists.
True ☐ False ☐

3. Nine out of ten countries with the lowest levels of religious practice are in Africa.
True ☐ False ☐

4. About three out of four Irish people say they pray to God at least once a week.
True ☐ False ☐

READ AND ANSWER!

Read the following story and answer all the questions that follow.

Changes in Religious Practice in Ireland since the 1950s

Jo: What was it like growing up in Ireland in the 1950s?

Mr Murphy: Things were very different then, compared to how they are today, in many ways.

Jo: What about religious practice – has that changed much since the 1950s?

Mr Murphy: The way people practise their religion has changed a lot. When I was young most people attended religious services every week. In my family we went to Mass every Sunday. The whole family would get up early and put on our best clothes. We would go without any breakfast because we had to fast before receiving Holy Communion. My mother and sisters always wore scarves on their heads when they went to religious services.

Jo: Did you enjoy going to religious services with your family every week?

Mr Murphy: Yes, I did. I enjoyed spending time with my family and it also gave me a chance to meet my friends and everyone in my parish. However, participating in religious services then was different to how it is today.

Jo: In what way was it different?

Mr Murphy: For a start, Mass was said in Latin which I did not understand so, as you can imagine, I found it very hard to be involved. The priest had his back to the people and they were not as involved in the prayers during Mass, whereas today when I go to Mass the priest is facing me, he is speaking a language that I can understand and I can be more actively involved.

Jo: Do you still go to religious services every week?

Mr Murphy: Yes, I do. I believe it is very important to be active in my parish and I still enjoy meeting my family and friends at religious services. Unfortunately I see less people at religious services each week and this makes me very sad.

1. From your reading of the above interview, outline two examples of changes in religious practice that have taken place in Ireland since the 1950s.

(i) ____

(ii) ____

2. Give **two** reasons why religious practice is important for people of religious faith.

(i) ____

(ii) ____

PART 2: THE BEGINNINGS OF FAITH

EXPLAIN IT!

1. Reflection means ________________________________

2. We experience awe and wonder when ________________________

3. A problem is ________________________________

4. A mystery is ________________________________

5. Atheism says ________________________________

6. Agnosticism says ________________________________

TICK THE BOX!

1. The question 'How are mountain ranges formed?' is an example of a mystery.
True ☐ False ☐

2. The Prophetic outlook applies to Hinduism and Buddhism.
True ☐ False ☐

3. The Humanist movement is an example of a religious source of meaning.
True ☐ False ☐

4. Humanists believe that there is no meaning of life to be discovered. They say that we each must make our own meaning.
True ☐ False ☐

LOOK AND ANSWER!

(*J/C 2003*)

This is a photograph of a young girl playing with balloons.

1. Pick one thing from the photograph which suggests that this is an experience of awe and wonder for the girl.

____

____

____

____

____

2. Some experiences that might make a person react with awe and wonder are birth, the beauty of nature and music. What does the expression 'awe and wonder' mean?

____

____

____

____

____

3. Experiences of awe and wonder make people ask questions about the meaning of life. Give examples of **two** such questions.

(i) ____

____

____

(ii) ____

____

____

READ AND ANSWER!

Read the following internet chat-room conversation and answer the questions that follow.

The Search for Meaning

Chris: Any suggestions about this question I'm working on for my Religious Education homework: Where do people find answers to questions about the meaning of life?

Dara: When I'm looking for answers to questions about life, I listen to music. Listening to the words of a song lets you hear what other people think about the meaning of life. What about you, Chris – what do you think?

Chris: I like music too, but you need to think about what you hear. You can't just take someone else's answers to questions about life. The words of songs can help, but you still need to think things through.

Pat: When I'm thinking about life I remember the way my granddad found meaning in the things he did. Even if it was just weeding a garden, or painting a wall, it made a difference and gave his life meaning.

Chris: I know what you mean. I feel my life has meaning when something I've done has made a difference to others.

Sam: Family and friends are important too, they make a difference to me and I make a difference to them.

Dara: Religion helps me to find answers. It helps me to make sense of life. Praying gives me time to think things out for myself.

Sam: I also think life is about facing challenges and overcoming them. That's what gives my life meaning.

Chris: I've got to sign off now. My homework won't write itself, you know! Thanks for all the help!

1. Outline **two** ways in which this conversation shows people searching for the meaning of life.

(i) ____

____

(ii) ____

____

2. **(a)** The term 'reflection' means ____

____

(b) Give **two** reasons why reflection can help people in their search for the meaning of life.

(i) ____

____

(ii) ____

____

3. Outline one way in which religion can help a person in his/her search for the meaning of life.

4. Family ☐ Friends ☐ Work ☐

Outline the way in which one of the above can help a person in his/her search for the meaning of life.

THINK ABOUT IT!

(J/C 2010)

Some experiences of life can give a person a sense of awe and wonder:

The beauty of nature ☐ The birth of a child ☐ The power of nature ☐

A. Explain how one such experience in life could make a person wonder and ask questions about the meaning of life.

B. Give **two** reasons why reflection is important for a person when searching for the meaning of life.

(i) ______________________________

(ii) ______________________________

C. In searching for answers to questions about the meaning of life, people sometimes turn to:

Family ☐ Friends ☐ Music ☐ Work ☐

Choose any two of the above and explain how each one can help people to find answers in their search for the meaning of life.

(i) ______________________________

(ii) ______________________________

PART 3: THE GROWTH OF FAITH

EXPLAIN IT!

1. Religious faith means ______________________________

2. An image of God is ______________________________

TICK THE BOX!

1. To trust someone means that you do not depend on him/her.

True ☐ False ☐

2. Jews, Christians and Muslims believe that religious faith is a gift from God.

True ☐ False ☐

3. Religious faith depends on our acceptance of the idea that there is more to life than meets the eye.

True ☐ False ☐

4. Jews, Christians and Muslims believe that our universe came into existence entirely by itself, without any action by God.

True ☐ False ☐

MATCH IT!

1. Match each explanation in column **B** with an image of God listed in column **A**. Fill in your answers in the spaces provided below.

A IMAGE OF GOD	B EXPLANATION
The 'Santa' God	An angry individual. He constantly watches over us. He only wants to catch us out. He punishes us when we offend him.
The 'Puppet Master' God	A source of comfort. He offers us a shoulder to cry on in difficult times. However, when things are going well in our lives, we ignore God.
The 'Stern Judge' God	A huge figure that looms over us. He controls everything that happens in our lives.
The 'Emergency Only' God	A nice old man with long white hair and beard. He sits on a throne up in the clouds. He is kind to those who please him.

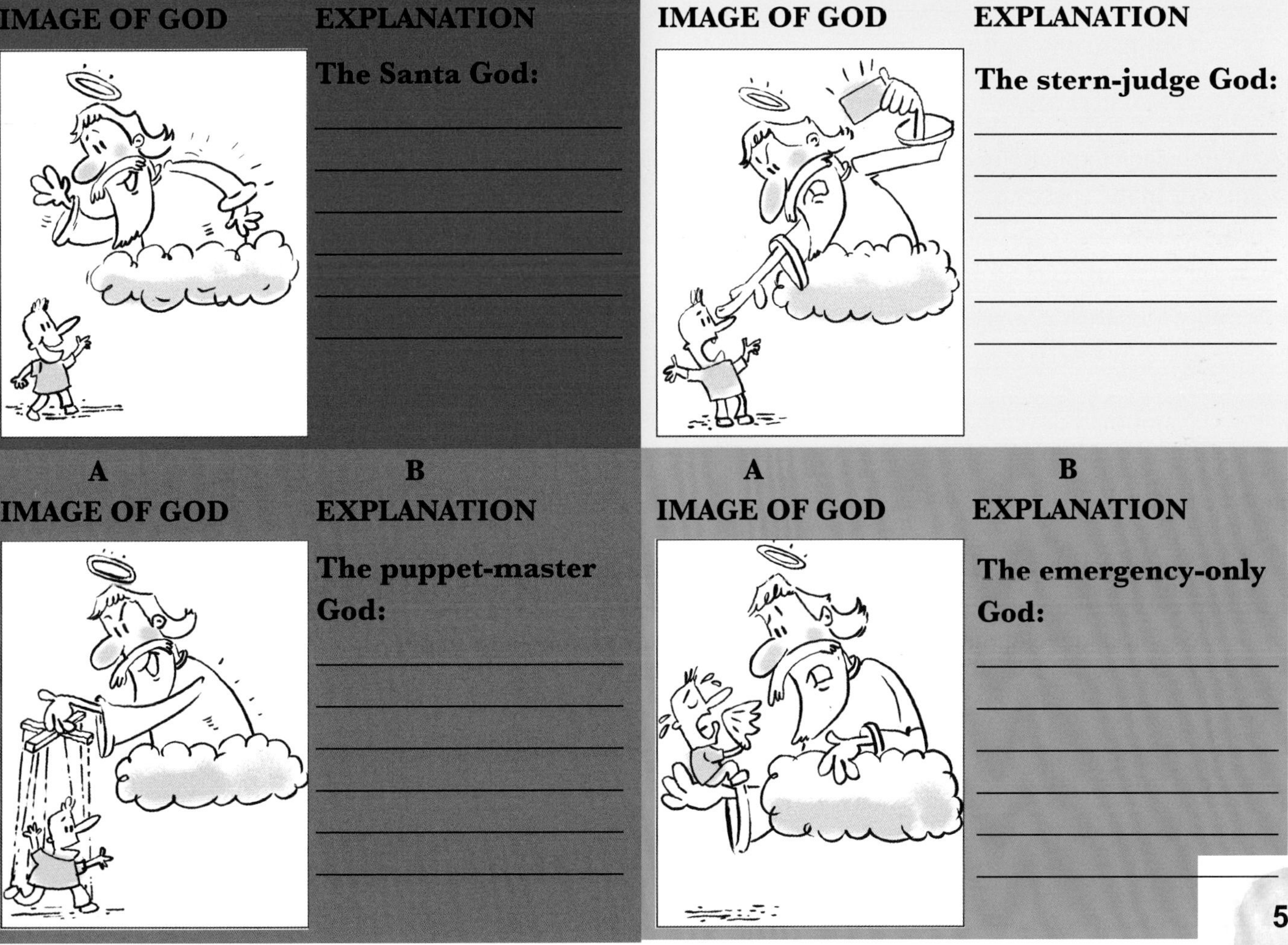

A
IMAGE OF GOD

B
EXPLANATION

The Santa God:

A
IMAGE OF GOD

B
EXPLANATION

The stern-judge God:

A
IMAGE OF GOD

B
EXPLANATION

The puppet-master God:

A
IMAGE OF GOD

B
EXPLANATION

The emergency-only God:

2. Match the different ways in which God acts in the world in column **B** with the correct person of the Trinity in column **A**. Fill in your answer in the spaces provided below.

A PERSON OF THE TRINITY	B WAY OF ACTING IN THE WORLD
God the Father	The one who gives life and strength to people
God the Son	The one who creates and sustains our world
God the Holy Spirit	The one who reveals himself out of love for human beings

A PERSON OF THE TRINITY	B WAY OF ACTING IN THE WORLD
God the Father	
God the Son	
God the Holy Spirit	

3. Match each explanation in column **B** with the correct type of development in column **A**. Fill in your answer in the spaces provided.

A TYPE	B EXPLANATION
Emotional development	Developing your faith in God
Intellectual development	Developing your character
Moral development	Developing your feelings
Spiritual development	Developing your mind

A TYPE	B EXPLANATION
Emotional development	
Intellectual development	
Moral development	
Spiritual development	

LOOK AND ANSWER!

(J/C 2010)

1. Pick **one** thing from this picture which suggests that it is based on an image of God.

2. State **two** things this image tells us about this child's understanding of God.
   (i)
   (ii)

3. Give two **other** examples of an image of God.
   (i)
   (ii)

READ AND ANSWER!

Read the following article and answer the questions below.

Friend to the Dying

Two men are walking along a beach covered in starfish washed up by the tide. The younger man picks one up to throw it back into the sea. The older one says 'Why bother? It won't make a difference.' The younger man looks down at the starfish he's holding. 'It'll make a difference to this one,' he says.

This little story inspired Phil, founder of several hospices, to provide care for terminally ill children and young adults. Phil has spent the last twenty years working with children who have severe disabilities or who are dying. Every day Phil comforts people who have to go through the greatest pain that life can dole out. 'It's the best way I know to live out my vocation,' Phil says.

Many people find Phil's warm smile and calm way reassuring. But how was Phil drawn to this vocation? 'Religion was a large part of my upbringing in Edinburgh,' Phil explains. 'My grandfather was very involved in our church. Later on, I worked in Great Ormond Street Hospital for Sick Children before moving to an adult ward in a nearby hospital. One of the patients I was looking after was a vicar who invited me to a service at her church. There I got to know people who had followed their vocation and had become members of a religious community.

'Some years later I was on a pilgrimage and suddenly I knew for certain that I should join a religious community. My family didn't like my decision and thought I would be wasting my life. But when Helen House was opened, the first ever place to offer special care for children who were dying, my mother appreciated what I was doing.

'Working in Helen House is not about being an expert,' Phil says. 'It's about companionship and kindness. After twenty-one years I have fewer answers to the big questions than I had at the outset. But what the experience of working with children has taught me is that, regardless of your belief or lack of it, when you're caring for people you are walking on holy ground.'

Adapted from: *The Sunday Times*

1. From your reading of this article outline two things that may have influenced Phil's religious belief.

____

____

____

____

2. Outline two ways in which Phil's life has been changed by his /her religious commitment.

(i) ____

(ii) ____

3. 'When you're caring for people you are walking on holy ground.' Explain in your own words what you think Phil means by this.

4. How does this article show what is meant by mature faith?

PART 4: THE EXPRESSION OF FAITH

EXPLAIN IT!

1. Ministry means

2. A volunteer is

READ AND ANSWER!

Read the following article and answer the questions below.

Understanding the Work of Samaritans

Samaritans was founded in 1953 by an Anglican priest named Chad Varah. He was the rector of St Stephen's church in London. The name of our organisation comes from the gospel parable of the Good Samaritan.

We are a non-religious charitable organisation. Our membership is open to people of all faiths and those who belong to none. Our vision (i.e. what motivates us to do what we do) can be summarised as follows:

We want to see a society in which fewer people die by suicide, where people are better able to explore their own feelings, where people are able to acknowledge and respect the feelings of others.

We offer a befriending service by trained volunteers. We provide emotional support to anyone in distress. We help victims of physical or sexual abuse as well as anyone who is at risk of suicide.

We believe that we must give people an opportunity to be heard. We treat all those who contact us with respect and take what they say seriously. This can help to alleviate (i.e. reduce) some of the despair and loneliness people feel.

We are not easily shocked. There is no problem that we will refuse to discuss.

All Samaritans are volunteers. We are not paid for what we do. We come from all walks of life. Usually, only members of our immediate families know that we are Samaritans. We are known to those who contact us only by a first name. Most contact is done by means of a twenty-four hour telephone helpline, but we also have a drop-in service at some locations.

All Samaritans must follow this strict set of rules:

- We guarantee complete confidentiality (i.e. secrecy) about the identity of a caller.
- We do not offer the caller a counselling service. You are not bombarded with any advice or 'message' by us. We provide a listening ear and an opportunity to talk through your problems, without fear of being either condemned or dismissed.
- If you talk to us (either by telephone or by dropping in to see us) you will not be contacted by us afterwards, unless you specifically ask us to do so.

There are over 200 branches of Samaritans in Ireland and the United Kingdom. If you need to talk, we are there to listen.

1. Who founded Samaritans? ______________________________

2. Where does the name Samaritans come from? ______________________________

____

3. What kind of ministry do Samaritan volunteers offer? ______________________________

____

4. Describe the membership of Samaritans.

____

____

____

____

5. What is the vision of Samaritans?

____

____

____

____

6. Describe the service offered by Samaritan volunteers.

7. What are the three strict rules all Samaritans must follow?

PART 5: CHALLENGES TO FAITH

EXPLAIN IT!

1. A worldview is

2. Tolerance means

3. Religious indifference means

4. Science is

5. The technological worldview says that

6. The creation is

7. Fundamentalism says that

TICK THE BOX!

1. Our universe began in a vast, cosmic explosion called the Big Bang.
   True ☐ False ☐

2. Developing your character is called intellectual development.
   True ☐ False ☐

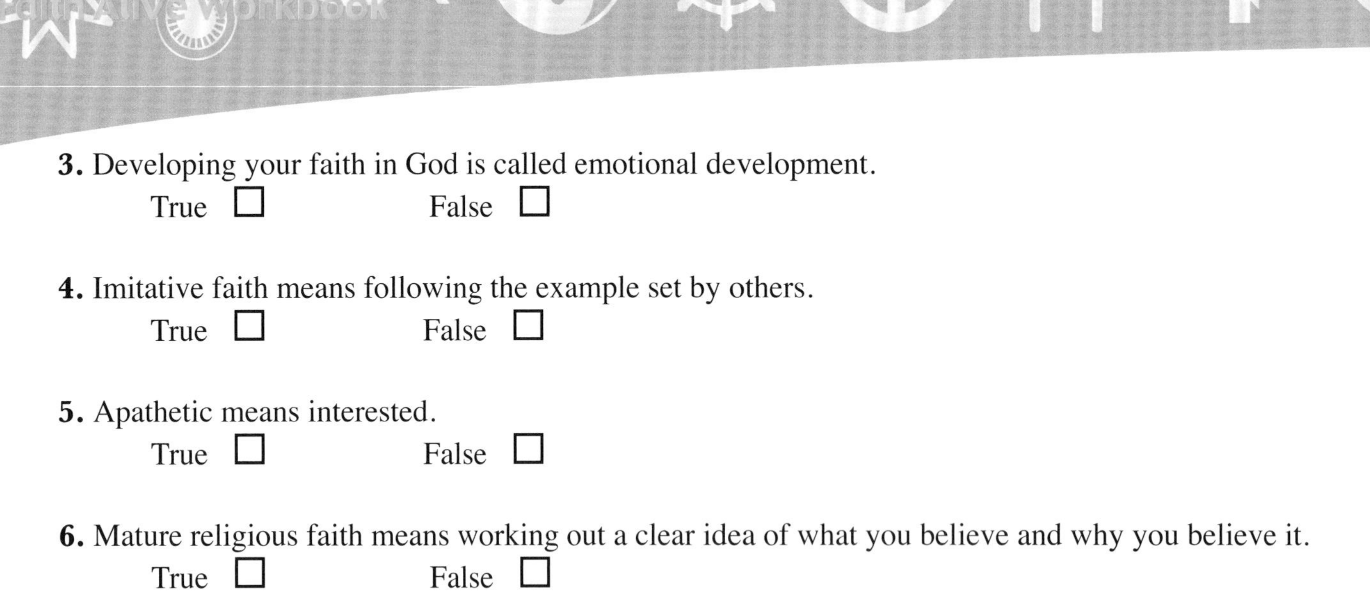

3. Developing your faith in God is called emotional development.
True ☐ False ☐

4. Imitative faith means following the example set by others.
True ☐ False ☐

5. Apathetic means interested.
True ☐ False ☐

6. Mature religious faith means working out a clear idea of what you believe and why you believe it.
True ☐ False ☐

7. In the secular worldview, if you have religious faith it should be considered an entirely private matter.
True ☐ False ☐

8. Materialism says that the only things that are really important are wealth, power and social status.
True ☐ False ☐

READ AND ANSWER!

Read the following article and answer all the questions that follow.

The Benefits of Religion

The first ever advertisement campaign to promote religious practice has been launched by the Iona Institute with the message, 'Here's a little science. The practice of religion is good for you.' This campaign consists of 110 bus shelter advertisements running over a fortnight throughout Dublin city.

David Quinn, director of the Iona Institute, says, 'This campaign is unprecedented. Nothing like it has ever taken place in Ireland, or anywhere else that we know of. There are now many scientific studies showing that religious practice has numerous beneficial effects. The aim of the campaign is to let people know about this.'

The campaign is based on a paper called **The Psycho-Social Benefits of Religious Practice** by well-known psychiatrist Professor Patricia Casey.

The paper examines various scientific studies carried out in this area which show that religious practice is associated, on average, with lower levels of depression, lower levels of marital breakdown, lower levels of alcohol and drug abuse, lower levels of pregnancy among teenagers, faster recovery from bereavement, faster recovery from illness and longer life expectancy.

The campaign invites people to examine the evidence through a dedicated website called www.religiouspractice.ie. David Quinn says, 'Religion has a very negative image at present. The campaign was first conceived four years ago when books like **The God Delusion** were bestsellers. We wanted to counter this negativity by pointing to the evidence that, on the whole, religious practice is beneficial for individuals and society.'

He emphasised the non-denominational nature of the campaign. 'The message of this campaign is not specific to any one denomination, or even any one religion. It is a generic message and applies to all the mainstream religions. This is why we asked the bishops from both the Catholic Church and from the Church of Ireland to write forewords to Professor Casey's paper last year.'

Adapted from: *cinews.ie* and *Dublin Examining Board* (2011)

1. From your reading of this article, outline one aim of this advertisement campaign.

2. What do the scientific studies referred to in this article claim about the benefits of religious practice on people's lives?

3. (**a**) What is a 'worldview'?

(**b**) Religion and science see the world from different points of view. How do you think this article might support the argument that religion and science **complement** each other?

4. Religious faith ☐ **Religious practice** ☐

How does this article show what is meant by **one** of the above?

5. Describe **one** way in which materialism could challenge a person's religious faith.

THINK ABOUT IT!

(J/C 2008)

1. Imagine you are doing a project on the creation of the world. Outline **two** points Christianity teaches about the creation of the world.

(i) ______________________________

____

(ii) ______________________________

____

2. Outline **two** points that science teaches about the creation of the world.

(i) ______________________________

____

(ii) ______________________________

____

3. Describe **one** similarity between what a religion says and what science says about the creation of the world.

____

____

____

____

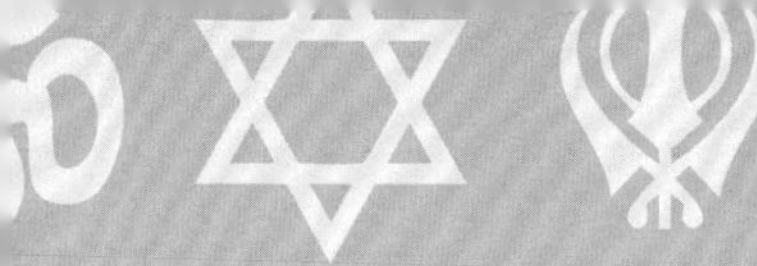

WORDSEARCH

Find the following key ideas:

AGNOSTICISM
ATHEISM
AWE
BELIEF
CREATION
EVOLUTION
FAITH
FUNDAMENTALISM
INDIFFERENCE
MATERIALISM
MYSTERY
PARTNERSHIP
PRACTICE
PROBLEM
REFLECTION
SECULARISM
THEISM
WONDER

F	Z	P	H	F	V	H	W	S	S	H	M	E	Y	Q
M	U	O	I	J	A	M	D	E	F	M	S	V	W	L
R	Q	N	I	H	E	I	C	F	S	T	I	O	B	N
T	H	W	D	L	S	U	T	I	X	H	L	L	Y	Y
M	G	L	B	A	L	R	C	H	W	E	A	U	R	G
P	S	O	F	A	M	I	E	O	H	I	I	T	E	M
Z	R	I	R	P	T	E	N	N	B	S	R	I	T	F
P	Q	I	E	S	R	D	N	Y	T	M	E	O	S	W
O	S	U	O	H	E	A	C	T	J	R	T	N	Y	W
M	F	N	I	R	T	C	C	Y	A	W	A	H	M	S
L	G	I	P	B	G	A	O	T	K	L	M	P	A	L
A	F	E	I	L	E	B	Y	K	I	W	I	S	D	N
I	N	D	I	F	F	E	R	E	N	C	E	S	O	Y
A	W	E	C	R	E	A	T	I	O	N	E	L	M	L
Y	C	N	O	I	T	C	E	L	F	E	R	U	H	S

SOLVE IT!

1 2 3 4 5 6 7 8 9 10 11 12 13

Clues

Across

3. Says there is no way to know whether or not there is a God.
7. Something we can figure out and solve.
8. Serving others by playing a constructive role in your community.
12. Means 'not caring.'
13. Means thinking about who you are and why you are here.

Down

1. Your general outlook on life.
2. Something you accept as true.
4. It wants a separation between religion and the state.
5. Someone who chooses to give up free time to help others.
6. The action of God that brought the universe into existence.
9. Something beyond our capacity to ever completely figure out and solve.
10. Says there is no God.
11. Knowledge of how the world works.

Section E

The Celebration of Faith

PART 1: THE WORLD OF RITUAL

EXPLAIN IT!

1. A place of religious significance is ______________________________

2. A sacred site is ______________________________

3. A pilgrimage is ______________________________

4. A shrine is ______________________________

5. An action of religious significance is ______________________________

6. Times of religious significance are ______________________________

TICK THE BOX!

1. A place of religious significance is also called a sacred site.
True ☐ False ☐

2. A pilgrimage can only be undertaken by a pilgrim travelling alone.
True ☐ False ☐

3. The River Ganges is a sacred place associated with which of the following world religions:
Buddhism ☐ Christianity ☐ Hinduism ☐ Judaism ☐ Islam ☐

4. An action which carries meaning for you, and is important to you, can be said to have significance.
True ☐ False ☐

5. When Hindus reach their sacred sites they bathe and pray that their sins will be washed away.
True ☐ False ☐

6. The name 'Jerusalem' means 'the city of the saints'.
True ☐ False ☐

7. The headquarters of the Catholic Church is located in the Vatican.
True ☐ False ☐

8. Croagh Patrick is a place of Christian pilgrimage because it was where a Marian apparition took place in 1879.

True ☐ False ☐

9. Advent is a time of preparation for Easter.

True ☐ False ☐

10. Christmas is a moveable feast.

True ☐ False ☐

11. Easter celebrates the resurrection of Jesus Christ.

True ☐ False ☐

MATCH IT!

1. Match each description given in column **B** with the place of pilgrimage listed in column **A**. Fill in your answers in the spaces provided.

A PLACE OF PILGRIMAGE	B DESCRIPTION
Ayodha, India	This contains the tomb of the Prophet Muhammad.
The Western Wall, Jerusalem, Israel	This contains a relic of the Buddha.
The Temple of the Tooth, Kandy, Sri Lanka	This was built on the site of the crucifixion, burial and resurrection of Jesus Christ.
The Church of the Holy Sepulchre, Jerusalem, Israel	This is the site of the Temple in which the ancient Jews worshipped God.
The Mosque in Madinah, Saudi Arabia	Hindus say that this was the birthplace of the god Rama.

A PLACE OF PILGRIMAGE	B DESCRIPTION
Ayodha, India	
The Western Wall, Jerusalem, Israel	
The Temple of the Tooth, Kandy, Sri Lanka	
The Church of the Holy Sepulchre, Jerusalem, Israel	
The Mosque in Madinah, Saudi Arabia	

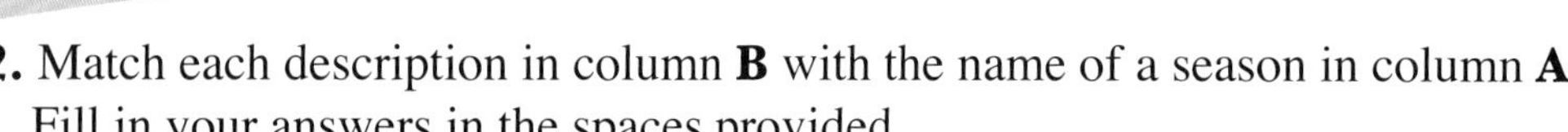

2. Match each description in column **B** with the name of a season in column **A**.
Fill in your answers in the spaces provided.

A **SEASONS OF THE CHURCH YEAR**	**B** **DESCRIPTION**
Advent	This is a time to reflect on Jesus Christ's message about the Kingdom of God.
Christmas	This celebrates the resurrection of Jesus Christ.
Ordinary Time	This is a time of preparation for Easter.
Lent	This is a time of preparation for Christmas.
Easter	This celebrates the birth of Jesus Christ.

A **SEASONS OF THE CHURCH YEAR**	**B** **DESCRIPTION**
Advent	
Christmas	
Ordinary Time	
Lent	
Easter	

LOOK AND ANSWER!

(*J/C 2004*)
This is a photograph of a Holy Week procession in Spain.

A. Identify **one** thing in this photograph which suggests that Holy Week is a time of significance.

____

____

____

B. Holy Week is a time of significance for which one of the following world religions?
Tick the correct box.
Buddhism ☐ Christianity ☐ Hinduism ☐ Judaism ☐ Islam ☐

C. Give **two** reasons why Holy Week is a time of significance in the world religion you have ticked above.
(i) ____

____

(ii) ____

____

THINK ABOUT IT!

(J/C 2010)

Lough Derg, County Donegal is a place of religious importance for members of one community of faith in Ireland.

A. Name **one** other place in Ireland that is important to members of a community of faith.

____

____

____

B. Give **two** reasons why the place you have named is important to a community of faith.
(i) ____

____

(ii) ____

____

C. Describe **one** way in which people worship in the place you have named above.

____

____

____

PART 2: THE EXPERIENCE OF WORSHIP

EXPLAIN IT!

1. Worship is ____

____

____

____

2. A religious ritual is ____

____

____

____

3. To participate in worship means ____

____

____

____

TICK THE BOX!

1. To worship is to show a lack of religious faith.
   True ☐ False ☐

2. Worship involves activities in which God is honoured.
   True ☐ False ☐

3. To call God the Supreme Being means that no one is as great as or greater than God.
   True ☐ False ☐

4. A ritual is an event where people use symbolic objects, words and actions to express what is deeply important to them.
   True ☐ False ☐

5. Catholics always perform wudu before they start to pray in a church.
   True ☐ False ☐

6. Liturgical worship is pulpit-centered.
   True ☐ False ☐

IDENTIFY THE PLACE OF WORSHIP!

Here are five places of worship. Match each picture with the correct religion listed in the spaces below.

RELIGIONS: Hinduism Judaism Buddhism Christianity Islam

PLACE OF WORSHIP		RELIGION
Mandir		
Synagogue		
Vihara		
Church		
Mosque		

PART 3: WORSHIP AS RESPONSE TO MYSTERY

[Higher Level Only]

EXPLAIN IT!

1. An encounter with mystery is ______________________________

____

____

2. Reflection means ______________________________

____

____

3. To experience wonder is ______________________________

____

____

4. A sacrifice is ______________________________

____

____

TICK THE BOX!

1. Religion began as an attempt by our earliest ancestors to understand the meaning and purpose of their lives.

True ☐ False ☐

2. Newgrange is a megalithic tomb.

True ☐ False ☐

3. The Jews were the first people to accept polytheism.

True ☐ False ☐

PART 4: SIGN AND SYMBOL

EXPLAIN IT!

1. A sign is ______________________________

____

2. A symbol is ______________________________

____

3. A religious identity consists of ______________________________

____

4. An icon is ______________________________

____

TICK THE BOX!

1. The celebration of the seven sacraments is most associated with which of the following world religions?

Buddhism ☐ Christianity ☐ Hinduism ☐ Judaism ☐ Islam ☐

2. A symbol has only one meaning.

True ☐ False ☐

3. A Christmas candle is a symbol.

True ☐ False ☐

4. An icon offers a life-like portrait.

True ☐ False ☐

5. The earliest known churches date from the first century CE.

True ☐ False ☐

6. Sacrament means 'a holy place'.

True ☐ False ☐

7. The sacraments of Baptism and Confirmation can be received only once.

True ☐ False ☐

8. Eucharist means 'thanksgiving'.

True ☐ False ☐

MATCH IT!

1. Match the correct explanation from column **B** with each sign listed in column **A**. Fill in your answers in the spaces provided.

A SIGN	B EXPLANATION	A SIGN	B EXPLANATION
M7	Slippery stretch of road ahead		Speed limit
	Youth hostel ahead	80 km/h	Entry to motorway
	Roundabout ahead	P	No left turn
Brú Óige YOUTH HOSTEL 1 km	No parking		

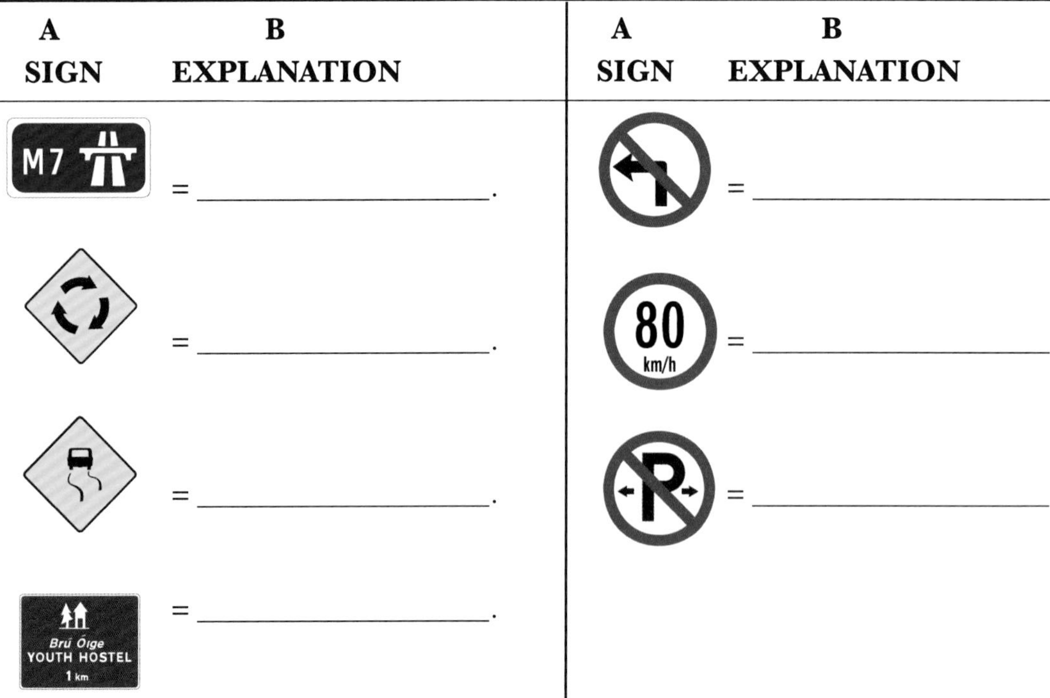

A SIGN	B EXPLANATION	A SIGN	B EXPLANATION
M7	= ____________________.		= ____________________.
	= ____________________.	80 km/h	= ____________________.
	= ____________________.	P	= ____________________.
Brú Óige YOUTH HOSTEL 1 km	= ____________________.		

2. Match the correct religion in column **B** with each religious symbol in column **A**. Fill in your answers in the spaces provided.

A SYMBOL	B RELIGION	A SYMBOL	B RELIGION
	Islam		Hinduism
	Buddhism		Christianity
	Judaism		

A SYMBOL	B RELIGION	A SYMBOL	B RELIGION
	= _____________.		= _____________.
	= _____________.		= _____________.
	= _____________.		

3. Match each explanation in column **B** with the correct gesture listed in column **A**.
Fill in your answers in the spaces provided.

A CHRISTIAN GESTURE	B MEANING
Kneeling	You want to be a peacemaker.
Standing	You recognise God's greatness and worship only God.
Blessing	You believe that Jesus rose from the dead.
Shaking hands	By tracing the symbol of the cross, you identify yourself as a Christian.

A CHRISTIAN GESTURE	B MEANING
Kneeling	
Standing	
Blessing	
Shaking hands	

LOOK AND EXPLAIN!

Identify each feature of this icon. Write your answers in the spaces provided.

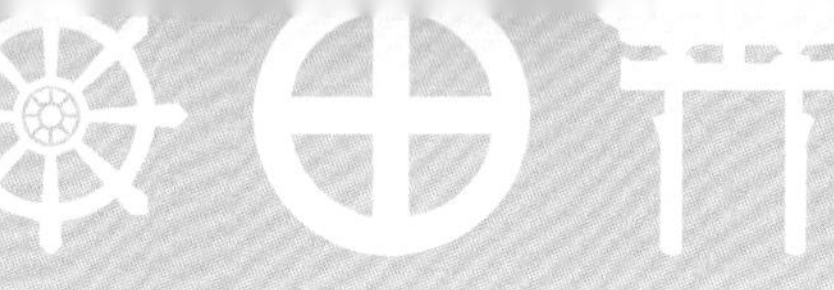

READ AND ANSWER!

Read the following extract from a letter and answer all the questions below.

Reflections on a Christmas Carol Service

I'm just back from the Christmas Carol Service. Even though it was cold, just about everyone was there. When we all stood to sing 'O Come All Ye Faithful' I thought of you; I know it's your favourite Christmas carol.

The children from the local school decorated a Christmas tree with special symbols. Each symbol stood for a person from the Bible who was looking forward to the coming of the Messiah. All the parents looked very proud watching their children place stars and harps on the branches of the tree. Two teenagers read a commentary about each of the people represented on this special tree, which is called a Jesse tree.

Rev Farrell read modern poems and prayers as well as readings from the Bible. The whole community was represented in the procession to put the figures into the crib. The figures of Mary and Joseph were carried by a newly married couple who have just moved here. I thought it was nice to include them in that way. Members of a local band even wrote their own carol for the occasion. You could see that it meant a lot to everyone.

We lit candles for friends and family members who weren't with us. I lit a candle for you, all those miles away. I didn't need to say anything. Just lighting the candle and watching the flame was enough for me to know that you would have a good Christmas too.

When I shook hands with people as a sign of peace, lots of people asked me to give you their best wishes and to wish you a happy Christmas. During the sign of peace the local youth group brought up boxes of toys and food which they had collected for people in need.

I hope you liked the present I sent you. I also included a tiny bit of straw from the crib. I'm sure you were wondering what it was. I thought it would remind you of all those you know who love you and who are thinking about you as they celebrate Christmas.

1. What evidence is there in this letter to suggest that Christmas is a time of religious importance?

____

____

____

____

2. (**a**) What evidence is there in this letter to show that the carol service was an example of communal prayer?

____

____

____

____

(**b**) Give **one** example of a symbol that was used during the carol service and explain what it means.

____

____

____

____

3. Give **two** reasons why people worship.

(i) ____________________

____

(ii) ____________________

____

4. How does this letter show what is meant by one of the following:

Religious belief ☐ Wonder ☐

____

____

____

____

____

____

____

PLACES OF WORSHIP

Identify the features indicated for each of the following places of Christian worship. Fill in your answers in the spaces provided below.

A. A Catholic Church

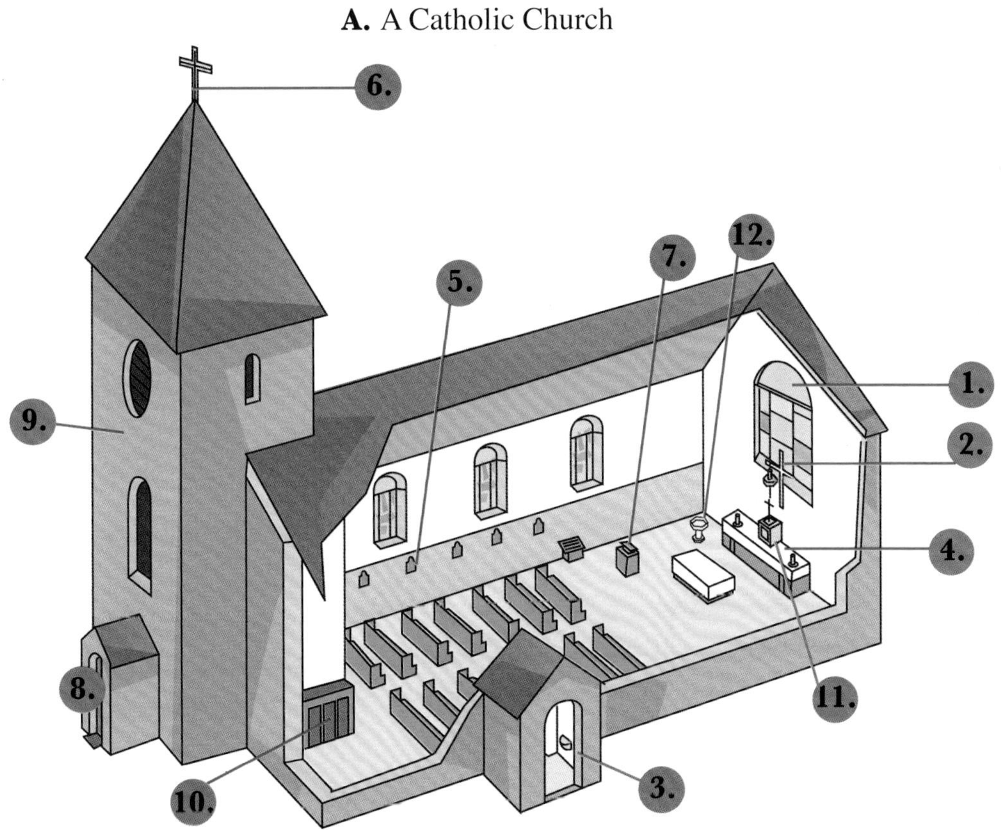

1. = ____________________.
2. = ____________________.
3. = ____________________.
4. = ____________________.
5. = ____________________.
6. = ____________________.
7. = ____________________.
8. = ____________________.
9. = ____________________.
10. = ____________________.
11. = ____________________.
12. = ____________________.

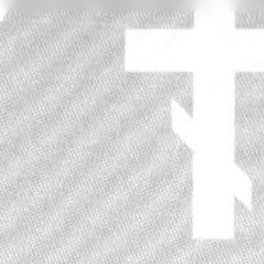

B. An Anglican Church

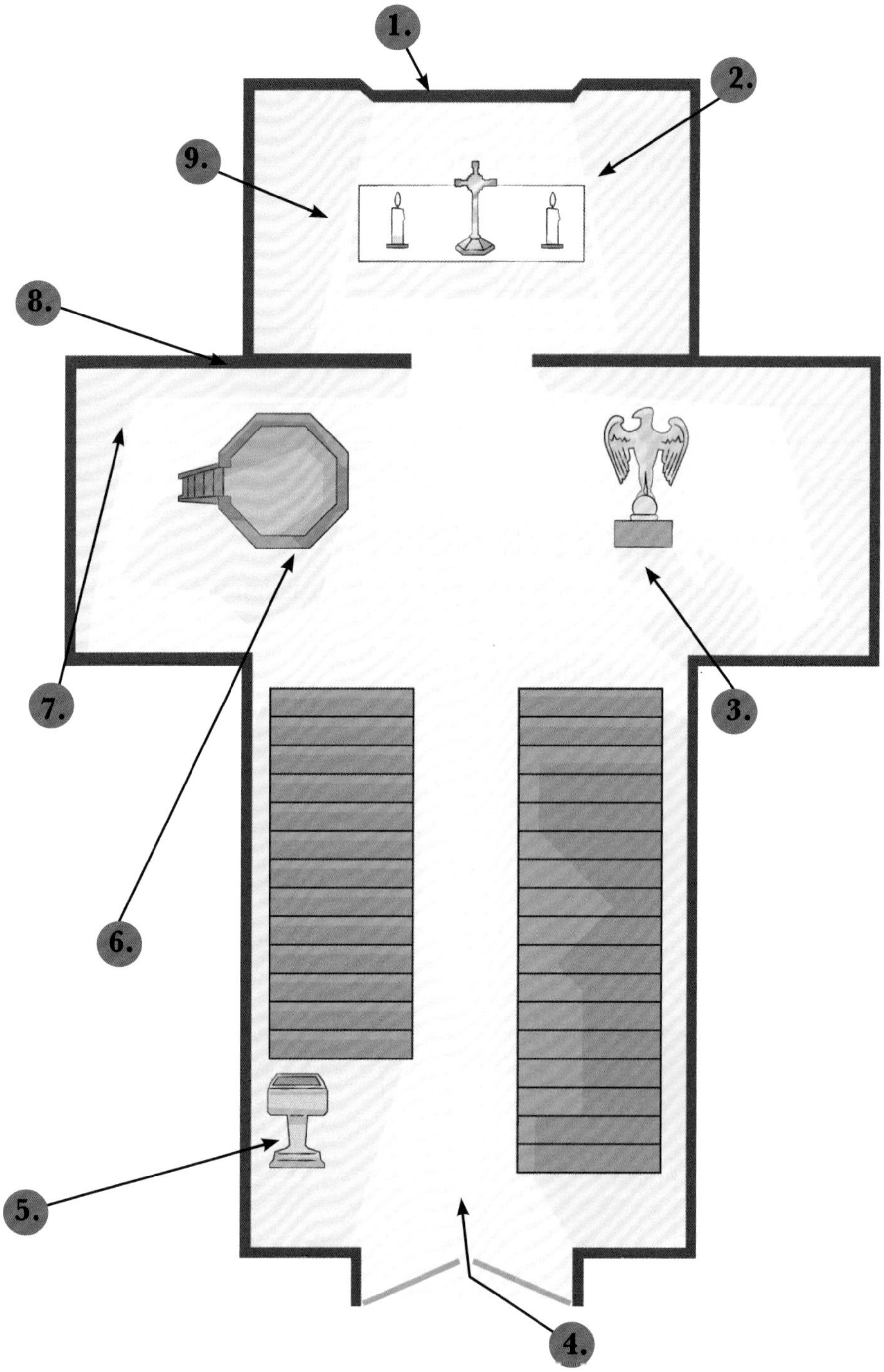

1. = ________________.
2. = ________________.
3. = ________________.
4. = ________________.
5. = ________________.
6. = ________________.
7. = ________________.
8. = ________________.
9. = ________________.

THINK ABOUT IT!

(J/C 2009)

Buddhism ☐ Christianity ☐ Hinduism ☐ Judaism ☐ Islam ☐

1. Tick **one** of the world religions above that you have studied. Name **one** symbol associated with the world religion you have ticked.

____

2. Describe the meaning of the symbol you have named for members of the world religion with which it is associated.

____

3. Give **two** reasons why people use symbols to express their religious faith.

(i) ______________________________

(ii) ______________________________

4. People have different ways of participating in worship – gestures, music, readings, etc. Explain how one way of participating in worship can help people to communicate with God.

____

PART 5: PRAYER

EXPLAIN IT!

1. Prayer is ______________________________

2. Meditation is ______________________________

TICK THE BOX!

1. Moses prayed and fasted for forty days and nights before receiving the Twelve Commandments.

True ☐ False ☐

2. Vocal prayer is silent prayer.

True ☐ False ☐

3. Personal prayer is when you join together with others to pray.

True ☐ False ☐

4. Contemplation is a type of silent prayer.

True ☐ False ☐

MATCH IT!

Match each explanation in column **B** with the correct type of prayer in column **A**. Fill in your answers in the spaces provided below.

A **TYPE OF PRAYER**	**B** **EXPLANATION**
Adoration	Ask God to help someone in need.
Intercession	Admit your sin. Learn from it and decide to do better in future.
Petition	Respond to something by praising God.
Penitence	Express gratitude to God for the things you take for granted.
Protection	Ask God for help or for the courage to endure some challenge.
Thanksgiving	Remember that God is there to guide you and that God's love is greater than the power of evil.

A **TYPE OF PRAYER**	**B** **EXPLANATION**
Adoration	
Intercession	
Petition	
Penitence	
Protection	
Thanksgiving	

LOOK AND ANSWER!

(J/C 2008)

This is a photograph of people using meditation during prayer.

1. Pick **one** thing from the photograph which shows that these people are using meditation.

____

____

2. What does the term 'meditation' mean in a religious tradition?

____

____

3. Give **two** reasons why people use meditation to pray.

(i) ____

____

(ii) ____

____

READ AND ANSWER!

Read the following letter and answer the questions below.

A Letter to God

Hi God,

It's me. I know you don't normally hear from me but my teacher asked me to drop you a line. It's all good though – I'm not my usual bored self! I'm just back from a retreat. I thought it would be boring, but everyone had to go so I went.

Well, I wasn't bored at all; it was great! We did all these group things that were really cool. Some of the talks we had were funny. Even when people got serious about things in

life, everyone was listening. We talked with each other in small groups about life and what is important to us. I said stuff I'd never said out loud before. What I found cool about the day was that people listened to what I said. They really showed consideration for me and I also listened hard to what they said about their lives. We all found out a lot about each other. There was a real sense of caring among the group. It sounds funny for me to be talking this way, but I have to say it was really good.

We also had quiet times during the retreat when nobody spoke and we could just think about our feelings and what we valued in life. During the prayer service, we listened to a song, 'Rejoice in the Lord Always'. Everyone was smiling a lot and the song really suited how we were feeling. Then we all had a chance to say things we liked about our lives. Lots of people remembered different things they were thankful for. Someone even mentioned that something I'd said was a help to them. I was really pleased that someone spoke so highly of what I had said. The things people were happy about just piled up and up and everybody just wanted to hear more and more.

I really enjoyed the retreat. I definitely wasn't bored.

Thank you God for all that happened.

Sam.

Source: Adapted from Saint Mary's Press

1. Reflection ☐ Respect ☐

Tick **one** of the above key ideas and outline how this letter shows what it means.

____

____

2. Give **one** reason why it is important for members of a community of faith you have studied to show respect.

____

____

____

3. Prayer of praise ☐ Prayer of thanksgiving ☐

Tick **one** of the above types of prayer that you have studied. Outline what is involved in the type of prayer you have ticked.

____

____

____

4. Prayer of praise ☐ Prayer of thanksgiving ☐

Outline how one of the above types of prayer can be seen in this letter.

____

____

____

5. State **two** reasons why people can find it difficult to pray.

(i) ____

____

(ii) ____

____

WORDSEARCH

CHURCH
CONTEMPLATION
HYMN
ICON
MANDIR
MEDITATION
MOSQUE
PILGRIMAGE
PRAYER
RITUAL
SACRAMENT
SACRED
SIGN
SYMBOL
SYNAGOGUE
VIHARA
WORSHIP

Y	G	M	A	N	D	I	R	C	K	N	X	L	R	C
Y	C	T	Y	Z	O	A	B	O	V	S	J	O	O	H
R	E	Y	A	R	P	U	V	N	P	W	D	B	K	U
M	J	M	E	D	I	T	A	T	I	O	N	M	D	R
A	O	D	Y	I	L	Z	S	E	T	D	L	Y	D	C
P	P	S	H	L	A	K	U	M	N	E	T	S	R	H
C	I	X	Q	R	S	G	D	P	E	B	R	C	Y	Q
P	T	L	A	U	O	H	P	L	M	H	A	J	F	F
N	I	H	G	G	E	S	H	A	A	A	Y	B	E	R
H	I	H	A	R	I	L	N	T	R	D	P	M	R	L
V	E	N	S	G	I	W	M	I	C	A	D	I	N	S
D	Y	U	N	R	C	M	M	O	A	E	T	P	C	U
S	T	Q	V	K	O	Q	A	N	S	U	E	K	J	Q
O	D	Z	K	Q	N	W	A	G	A	Y	Z	C	B	Q
A	I	D	E	R	C	A	S	L	E	Z	N	I	O	D

SOLVE IT!

Clues

Across

4. Underground tombs beneath Rome.

6. Someone who goes on a pilgrimage.

8. Birthplace of the Hindu god Rama.

14. Where Mary the Mother of Jesus is said to have appeared to Bernadette Soubirous in 1858.

15. Our way of organising the year.

16. It means 'thanksgiving' for Christians.

19. A richly decorated religious image painted on a wooden board.

Down

1. Name means 'the City of Peace'.

2. Period of preparation for the celebration of Christ's resurrection.

3. Offering something you believe is valuable to God.

5. It communicates more than one idea.

7. It means 'a holy mystery'.

8. Period of preparation for the celebration of Christ's birth.

9. A way of focusing your attention on and communicating with God.

10. The worship of anyone or anything other than God.

11. A mosque is built there. It contains the tomb of the Prophet Muhammad.

12. A monument that commemorates an important religious event.

13. A way to find inner peace so that you can focus on something important.

17. A building designed and used by Christians for worship.

18. It communicates one and only one idea.

Section F
The Moral Challenge

PART 1: INTRODUCTION TO MORALITY

EXPLAIN IT!

1. A choice is ______________________________

2. Morality is ______________________________

____

3. Human rights are ______________________________

4. Relationships are ______________________________

____

TICK THE BOX!

1. Morality is concerned with actions that are free, deliberate and informed.
True ☐ False ☐

2. Responsible means that you must answer for what you say or do.
True ☐ False ☐

3. Saying human rights are universal means they only apply to some people.
True ☐ False ☐

LOOK AND ANSWER!

HIT-AND-RUN KILLER HUNTED

(*J/C 2004*) This is a photograph of a newspaper headline describing a road accident in which the driver of a car killed a person and drove away.

1. State **one** way in which the situation described in this headline shows the need for respect.

____

____

2. State **two** ways in which the driver could be affected by his/her decision to drive away.

(i) ______________________________

____

(ii) ______________________________

____

3. Identify **two** ways in which a community could be affected by the driver's decision to drive away.

(i) ______________________________

____

(ii) ______________________________

____

PART 2: SOURCES OF MORALITY

EXPLAIN IT!

1. A value is ______________________________

____

2. Socialisation is ______________________________

____

3. The sources of our values are ______________________________

____

4. A code is ______________________________

____

5. A law is ______________________________

____

6. The common good is ______________________________

____

7. A religious moral vision is ______________________________

____

8. An authority is ______________________________

____

TICK THE BOX!

1. Learning means gaining the knowledge and skills you need to function as a member of society.
True ☐ False ☐

2. An informal code is one imposed on us by the community we live in.
True ☐ False ☐

3. Legal means something forbidden by law.
True ☐ False ☐

4. The Code of Hammurabi was based on the idea of 'an eye for an eye'.
True ☐ False ☐

5. The Magisterium of the Catholic Church consists of the pope and the college of bishops under his leadership.

True ☐ False ☐

MATCH IT!

Match each explanation in column **B** with the correct commandment in column **A**. Fill in your answers in the spaces provided.

A **THE TEN COMMANDMENTS**	B **EXPLANATION**
You shall worship the Lord your God, and Him only shall you serve.	Never tell lies, commit perjury or spread gossip.
You shall not take the name of the Lord your God in vain.	Help, obey and respect your parents.
Remember to keep holy the Sabbath day.	Do not be jealous of other people's success or envious of their possessions.
Honour your father and your mother.	Have self-control and only have sexual intercourse within marriage.
You shall not commit murder.	Be faithful to your marriage partner in all you say and do.
You shall not commit adultery.	Respect God's name and do not use abusive language.
You shall not steal.	Put God first in your life, before everything else – especially wealth, power and pleasure.
You shall not bear false witness against your neighbour.	Worship God and respect his holy day by keeping it special.
You shall not covet your neighbour's spouse.	Never do anything that would harm or kill an innocent person.
You shall not covet anything that belongs to your neighbour.	Do not steal or damage the property of others. Do not cheat them out of what is rightfully theirs.

A THE TEN COMMANDMENTS	B EXPLANATION
You shall worship the Lord your God, and Him only shall you serve.	
You shall not take the name of the Lord your God in vain.	
Remember to keep holy the Sabbath day.	
Honour your father and your mother.	
You shall not commit murder.	
You shall not commit adultery.	
You shall not steal.	
You shall not bear false witness against your neighbour.	
You shall not covet your neighbour's spouse.	
You shall not covet anything that belongs to your neighbour.	

LOOK AND ANSWER!

(*J/C 2006*)

The Ten Commandments are as follows:

1. You shall worship the Lord your God, and Him only shall you serve.
2. You shall not take the name of the Lord your God in vain.
3. Remember to keep holy the Sabbath day.
4. Honour your father and your mother.
5. You shall not commit murder.
6. You shall not commit adultery.
7. You shall not steal.
8. You shall not bear false witness against your neighbour.
9. You shall not covet your neighbour's spouse.
10. You shall not covet anything that belongs to your neighbour.

Commandments **1–3** say what it means to love God.
Commandments **4–10**
deal with how we should love and respect one another.

This drawing shows a moral code.

1. Explain why this is an example of a moral code.

____

____

____

2. Name another religious moral code.

____

3. Give **two** reasons why a moral code is important in a community of faith.

(i) ____

____

____

____

(ii) ____

____

____

____

PART 3: GROWING IN MORALITY

EXPLAIN IT!

1. Moral maturity is ____
____
____

2. Moral immaturity is ____
____
____

TICK THE BOX!

1. Moral immaturity is where you do not accept your responsibilities as a member of your community.
True ☐ False ☐

2. Perjury means to tell the truth while under oath.
True ☐ False ☐

3. Guilt is a lack of awareness that you have done something wrong.
True ☐ False ☐

4. Someone with an informed conscience obeys rules without question.
True ☐ False ☐

5. Someone with a lax conscience acts in morally immature and selfish ways.
True ☐ False ☐

LOOK AND ANSWER!

(J/C 2008)

This is a photograph of people showing concern about a moral issue.

1. Pick **one** thing from the photograph which shows that these people are concerned about a moral issue.

2. Describe **one** other way in which people can show concern about a moral issue.

THINK ABOUT IT!

(J/C 2008)

1. Outline what the term 'conscience' means.

2. (i) Explain how a person's religious faith could influence his/her conscience.

(ii) Apart from religious faith, explain how **one** other factor could influence a person's conscience.

3. Describe **one** way in which a person's conscience can develop as he/she grows older.

PART 4: RELIGIOUS MORALITY IN ACTION

EXPLAIN IT!

1. A moral decision is ______________________________

2. Integrity means ______________________________

3. Justice means ______________________________

4. To sin means ______________________________

5. Moral evil is ______________________________

6. Justice means ______________________________

7. Forgiveness is ______________________________

8. The afterlife means ______________________________

9. Sacred means ______________________________

10. A steward is ______________________________

TICK THE BOX!

1. Honesty means being fair and keeping your promises.
   True ☐ False ☐

2. When a person acts with integrity, he or she behaves in a way that is dishonest.
   True ☐ False ☐

3. Fairness means treating everyone equally.
   True ☐ False ☐

4. To pardon, show mercy or compassion are examples of forgiveness.
   True ☐ False ☐

5. War is armed conflict between friendly groups.
True ☐ False ☐

6. A pacifist believes that all forms of physical violence are justified.
True ☐ False ☐

7. The environment is our world and everything in it.
True ☐ False ☐

MATCH IT!

1. These are questions you should ask yourself before making an important moral decision.

Match each question in column **B** with the correct stage in decision-making listed in column **A**. Fill in your answers in the spaces provided.

A STAGES IN DECISION-MAKING	B QUESTIONS TO ASK YOURSELF
Situation	What do I want to achieve?
Information	How will my action affect other people?
Guidance	Why am I doing this?
Aim	What exactly is the problem facing me?
Motive	Where can I get reliable advice?
Method	Do I have all the relevant facts?
Impact	What is the best way to achieve this?

A STAGES IN DECISION-MAKING	B QUESTIONS TO ASK YOURSELF
Situation	
Information	
Guidance	
Aim	
Motive	
Method	
Impact	

2. Match each statement in column **B** with the correct term listed in column **A**. Fill in your answers in the spaces provided.

A PEOPLE MAY BELIEVE THAT THE MORALITY OF AN ACTION DEPENDS ON...	B THIS CAN BE EXPRESSED AS...
Emotion	'I was only following orders.'
Common practice	'I was afraid I'd lose my job over it.'
Authority	'It seemed like the right thing to do at the time.'
The situation	'I felt really good about doing it.'
The consequences	'You can't do that, it's a crime.'
The law of the state	'Jesus said that we should always be willing to forgive.'
The teaching of a religion	'Don't worry, everyone is doing it.'

A PEOPLE MAY BELIEVE THAT THE MORALITY OF AN ACTION DEPENDS ON...	B THIS CAN BE EXPRESSED AS...
Emotion	
Common practice	
Authority	
The situation	
The consequences	
The law of the state	
The teaching of a religion	

READ AND ANSWER!

(J/C 2011)

Read the following extract and answer all the questions that follow.

Being a Steward

I recently visited a farm run by a religious order. It was a great experience. We were shown all the animals on the farm and how crops are being grown without using chemicals. After the tour of the farm we went to a meeting room where the people who work on the farm talked with us about how they enjoyed living close to nature. They spoke about the way Jesus treated everyone with care and respect and the duty we all have to care for the plant, animal and human life around us. They welcome visitors to their farm so as to encourage people to live in a way that respects all the forms of life that exist in the world today. They also showed us pictures about how the earth is being polluted and people are dying of hunger.

I was shocked to see how much damage can be done when people do not take care of the earth that has been given to us. From what we were shown on the farm you could clearly see how the behaviour of each person has an effect on others. Before we left the farm we talked about how each of us could use our own talents in a way that respects all forms of life and makes the earth a better place for everyone, i.e. planting trees, giving to charity, etc.

1. Outline how the connection between either actions and consequences **or** rights and responsibilities can be seen in the above extract.

____

____

____

____

____

____

2. In religious traditions the term 'stewardship' involves:

____

____

____

____

____

____

3. Describe **two** examples of how people practising stewardship can be seen in the above extract.

(i) ____

____

____

____

(ii) ____

____

____

____

4. Outline **two** ways in which a person's religious faith could encourage stewardship.

(i) ____

____

____

____

(ii) ____

____

____

____

THINK ABOUT IT!

(J/C 2011)

Family ☐ Friends ☐ School ☐

1. Choose **two** of the above and outline how each could influence a person's idea of what is right and wrong.

(i)

(ii)

2. Tick **one** of the following major world religions that you have studied:
Buddhism ☐ Christianity ☐ Hinduism ☐ Islam ☐ Judaism ☐

(a) Name **one** moral code associated with the world religion that you have ticked.

(b) Describe **one** way in which a moral code could guide a person when making a moral decision.

(c) Outline what is involved in another two stages of the process a person would go through in making a moral decision.

(i)

(ii)

(J/C 2010)

3. **(a)** Outline the understanding of forgiveness found in the teaching of one major world religion that you have studied.

(**b**) State **two** reasons why reconciliation is seen as important by the members of a world religion.

(**i**) ______________________________

(**ii**) ______________________________

(**c**) Describe **one** way in which one world religion offers its members an opportunity for reconciliation.

____

PART 5: LAW AND MORALITY

EXPLAIN IT!

1. A state is ______________________________

2. A law is ______________________________

3. A constitution is ______________________________

4. Religious fundamentalism says ______________________________

5. Pluralism says ______________________________

6. Libertarianism says ______________________________

TICK THE BOX!

1. In religious traditions freedom is when you are told what to do and how to think.
True ☐ False ☐

2. The constitution of a state is a document outlining the important political ideas and values on which the state is founded.
True ☐ False ☐

3. Secularism says that the laws of a country should be based on the moral vision of one particular religion.
True ☐ False ☐

4. Pluralism holds the view that all groups within a society have a right to carry out their religious and cultural practices.
True ☐ False ☐

THINK ABOUT IT!

(*J/C 2007*)

1. Give **one** example of a situation where there could be conflict between a country's laws and a particular religion.

____

____

____

____

____

2. Tick **one** of the boxes below and outline how it sees the relationship between a country's law and a religion.
Pluralism ☐ Religious fundamentalism ☐

____

____

____

____

____

WORDSEARCH

Find the following key ideas:

ACTION
CODE
CONSCIENCE
DECISION
GOLDEN RULE
LAW
LIBERTARIANISM
MAGISTERIUM
MORALITY
PEACE
PLURALISM
RIGHTS
SACRED
STEWARD
THEOCRACY
VALUE
VISION

L	A	C	T	I	O	N	C	A	H	L	D	P	C	P
K	I	L	B	H	Q	T	O	H	M	B	E	L	W	K
M	T	B	W	D	N	E	D	H	A	A	C	N	S	U
M	S	N	E	O	P	S	E	R	C	E	I	S	Y	Q
S	F	I	I	R	T	M	M	E	E	C	S	T	H	Y
G	T	S	L	L	T	O	Y	L	W	N	I	H	O	H
D	I	E	W	A	R	A	U	J	I	E	O	G	Z	T
V	E	W	W	A	R	R	R	Y	J	I	N	I	J	G
L	R	R	L	A	N	U	N	I	Q	C	L	R	M	P
F	C	I	C	E	R	C	L	T	A	S	N	A	B	B
G	T	J	D	A	C	D	A	P	R	N	R	J	W	N
Y	A	L	W	W	S	D	I	K	I	O	I	J	R	W
K	O	E	U	L	A	V	P	B	L	C	J	S	Y	F
G	O	R	G	Y	C	A	R	C	O	E	H	T	M	Z
M	A	G	I	S	T	E	R	I	U	M	Z	Y	B	M

SOLVE IT!

Clues

Across

5. Things all humans need in order to live full lives.
9. To choose freely to do what you know is wrong.
11. To let go of the anger and hate you feel towards another.
13. Where we are all treated equally.
14. Advice about what you should do.
16. His code offered the earliest and most complete set of laws known.
17. Letter written by the Pope giving advice to Catholics.
19. Staying true to your beliefs and doing what you believe is right.
20. The world and everything in it.

Down

1. God gave Moses ten of them.
2. Getting what you are entitled to.
3. Someone who cares for the earth.
4. A community of people organised under a government.
5. You must answer for what you say and do.
6. The capacity to apply your knowledge and values and decide what is the right thing to do.
7. Set of standards used to judge whether an action is right or wrong.
8. Means life after death.
10. An Irish word meaning 'compassion.'
12. The way we learn what is right and wrong.
15. Permitted by law.
18. Decision either to do or not do something.

THE JOURNAL BOOKLET

PART 1: AN INTRODUCTION TO JOURNAL WORK

AIMS

Journal work gives you the opportunity to:

- Encounter religion as a living reality in your community.
- Explore an area of personal interest.
- Develop a range of skills, such as research, observation, analysis and reflection.

MARKS

Your journal work is worth 100 marks, i.e. 20 per cent of the total marks awarded to Religious Education in the Junior Certificate examination.
This applies to both Higher Level and Ordinary Level.

STRUCTURE

The journal booklet itself is divided into five sections.
You must complete each section.

TITLES

Two titles are given for each of the six sections of the syllabus.
You have twelve possible titles to choose from.
You must submit your journal work on one of these titles.
The titles examined vary from year to year.
The titles are the same for both Higher Level and Ordinary Level.

CHOICES

You can choose to work either on your own or as part of a class group.
However, if you choose to work as part of a class group, you must do two things:

- Complete and submit your own individual journal booklet for assessment.
- Clearly set out your personal contribution to the group's work.

SKILLS

To complete your journal booklet, you will have to develop and use a number of skills.

KEY IDEA

A **skill** is an ability to do something or to complete some task.

These are the types of skills that are involved in completing the journal booklet:

- **Enquiry:** You learn how to ask relevant and useful questions about people, places and organisations.
- **Observation:** You learn how to listen to people when they are speaking, so that you can accurately record what they have said. You learn how to pay attention to what you are reading, so that you can pick out the important points.
- **Problem-solving:** You learn how to identify and anticipate problems involved in your work. Then you learn how to find solutions to them.
- **Research:** You learn how to find information that is relevant to your chosen topic.
- **Organisation:** You learn how to plan and organise your time effectively. You make sure to complete your journal work on time.

PART 2: SAMPLE JOURNAL BOOKLET

Coimisiún na Scrúduithe Stáit
State Examinations Commission

Junior Certificate Examination

Religious Education Journal Booklet

Total Marks: 100

General Directions for Candidates

1. Write your EXAMINATION NUMBER in this box: X
2. YEAR of submission:
3. WRITE ALL ANSWERS INTO THIS BOOKLET.
4. YOU MUST ATTEMPT ALL FIVE SECTIONS IN THIS BOOKLET.

For the Examiner only

NB

Please indicate the level at which the candidate took the examination. Ordinary Level ☐

(Please tick ✓ the correct box) Higher Level ☐

Note: Transfer Mark for Journal to grid of examination answer booklet.

	Mark
SECTION ONE	
SECTION TWO	
SECTION THREE	
SECTION FOUR	
SECTION FIVE	
Mark for Journal	

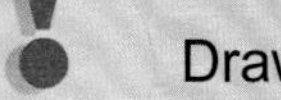

REMEMBER!
Draw any diagram/illustration directly on to a page of the journal booklet. Do not attach or affix any material to a page of the journal booklet.

12 marks

SECTION ONE

INTRODUCTION

GROUP / INDIVIDUAL

Did you do journal work on your own or as part of a group? (Tick ✓ the correct box)

Tick the correct box

Journal work on my own ☐ *Journal work as part of a group* ☐

TITLE

The title I chose for journal work is… Choose one title from the official list.

Write down the exact wording from this list.

The personal title of my journal work is…

Give your own interpretation of the official title. Use plain language here.

(2 marks)

I chose this title because… Give at least two reasons for your choice. Did you become interested in it because of a magazine article, book, documentary film, guest speaker or radio interview? Was it because of some personal concern or experience?

(4 marks)

BEGINNING

By doing journal work on this title I hoped to… You may answer in any of the following ways:

What did you hope to achieve by doing journal work on this title?

- Find out more about…
- Explore the reasons why…
- Better understand the role of…
- Discover what 'X' has in common with…

(6 marks)

12 marks

SECTION TWO

GETTING STARTED

PREPARING

To prepare for doing my journal work I... In this section, you must give a detailed

Consider for example: description of how you planned to complete your journal work.

What problems did you face in planning to do journal work on this title?

- Was it easy to find information on your chosen title?
- Did you have internet access?
- Does your school have a library?

What assignments did you plan to carry out?

- I hoped to visit...
- I tried to arrange an interview with...
- I decided to send an email to ... to ask for information about...

What research did you plan to conduct?

- I planned to conduct a class survey about...
- I asked for permission to invite a guest speaker...

What people did you plan to contact/ interview?

- A local religious leader (e.g. priest, rector, imam or rabbi).
- A college lecturer.
- An author on that subject.

What arrangements/ plans did you make for visits or events?

- I found out the opening times for...
- I arranged a time for an interview with...
- I wrote a letter inviting ... to speak to our class group.

Etc.

(12 marks)

24 marks

SECTION THREE

WORK

DESCRIBING

To do my journal work I…

Consider for example:

What work did you actually do to complete your journal on this title?

If you did your journal work as part of a group, remember to also outline the work done by the rest of the group.

What assignments were completed, events attended or activities organised, as part of your journal work?

Etc.

State three things you actually did as you researched and wrote on your chosen title. Be sure to link everything you say back to this title.

If you worked on your own:

- I carried out an internet search on…
- I sent an email to…
- I went to the local library and used its catalogue to find a book/article on…
- I kept detailed notes about what I found out about…

If you worked as part of a group:

- I helped to divide up the different tasks among the members of my group.
- I helped to draft the questions that we put to our guest speaker.
- I met the guest speaker when he/she arrived at our school.
- I introduced our guest speaker to our class.
- I recorded the guest speaker's answers to our questions.

(12 marks)

SECTION THREE

WORK *(continued)*

I included this in my journal work because ...

Why were these assignments/events/activities included as part of your journal work?

Say why you chose to do these particular things. How did they help you to better understand your title area? Did you visit somewhere you had never been before? Did you meet someone of a particular faith community for the first time? Did you learn more about the role...plays?

(6 marks)

YOUR REACTION

My reaction to doing this work was...

What was your first reaction to these assignments /events/ activities? → Be positive! How much did you know about this before starting work?

What part did you find most interesting? Why? → Explain how you were helped to better understand your title area.

What part did you find hardest? Why? → Did you find research straightforward or challenging? What skills did you develop doing it? How will these skills be useful in the future?

If you were working as part of a group what was your group's first reaction to these assignments/ events/activities? → Did everyone share your reaction? How did you work as a group? Did you encounter any difficulties?

How was this similar to or different from your own reaction?

Etc.

(6 marks)

42 marks

SECTION FOUR

DISCOVERIES

LEARNING

I learned... State three or four main points of information you have discovered.

Consider for example:

What did you learn from working on this title for your journal?

(10 marks)

As a result of what I have learned I will... Be positive!

Consider for example:

How have you been affected by doing journal work on this title?

Do you have a different attitude?

Do you have a different opinion?

Etc.

Has your attitude to the title changed since you began work on it?

Have you become better informed?

Are you more tolerant and respectful of other points of view?

Do you have a greater awareness of the constructive role religion can play in people's lives?

Do you have a greater understanding of the common ground between the world's religions?

(10 marks)

SECTION FOUR

DISCOVERIES *(continued)*

SKILLS Remember to choose two skills

Tick ✓ **two** of the following skills used in your journal work and explain how you used these skills.

Enquiry skills ☐ Observational skills ☐ Problem-solving skills ☐ Research skills ☐

Reflective skills ☐ Organisational skills ☐ Evaluation skills ☐

i. *I used* Research *skills*

when I...

- Used an internet search to locate information I needed to complete my journal work.
- Went to my local library and used its catalogue to locate articles and books I needed.
- Had an interview with ... and asked questions to get information I needed.

(5 marks)

ii. *I used* Organisational *skills*

when I... As an individual:

- Joined the local library in order to get access to its facilities.
- Arranged an interview with ... to get the information I needed to complete my journal.

As a member of a group:

- Planned for my group to visit...
- Wrote and sent a letter inviting our guest speaker.

In both cases:

- Used my organisational skills to record, structure and produce a report on my chosen title.

(5 marks)

SECTION FOUR

DISCOVERIES (continued)

LINKING

What topics /themes studied in your Religious Education course over the last three years, relate to what you discovered in journal work?

i. *My journal work reminded me of studying...*

because...

Give reason here.

Remember the six sections of the syllabus:

Section A: Communities of Faith
Section B: Christianity
Section C: Major World Religions
Section D: The Question of Faith
Section E: The Celebration of Faith
Section F: The Moral Challenge

(6 marks)

ii. *My journal work reminded me of studying...*

because...

Give reason here.

When writing your answers to parts (i) and (ii), keep in mind the key ideas of each section of the syllabus, e.g. inspiring vision / justice / stewardship / symbol and so on.

You must show the links between your journal title and two other sections of the syllabus.

(6 marks)

10 marks

SECTION FIVE

LOOKING BACK

REFLECTING

Looking back at my experience of doing journal work on this title…

Consider for example:

What do you think went well in your journal work?
- What was the best part of doing the journal?
- Did you build on existing skills and/or develop new ones?

If you were starting again, would you do journal work on this title differently?
- Would you approach the title in the same way as before?
- Would you do things differently?
- Where would you start looking for information this time?
- Would you work on your own or as part of a group?

Imagine someone in your school is starting out on journal work and has chosen the same title as you.
- Make recommendations.
- Where would you advise someone to start looking for information?

What advice would you give?
- Would you advise working as an individual or as part of a group?
- How should the work be divided up among the members of a group?
- How early should work on the journal title begin?
- How should a guest speaker be treated?
- How should a field trip be organised?

Etc.

(10 marks)

Notes

Notes

Notes